dejunk

Less of you and more of God

Gary Lacey

Dejunk

Published by GL London

All Bible quotations from

The Holy Bible: New International version, 1973,1978,1984, The International Bible society

The English Standard Version, By Harper Collins Publishers 2001 By Crossway Bibles, A division of Good news publishers

The message Bible in contemporary language, Copyright © 2002, 2010, By Eugene Peterson

Other Quotations

Soren kierkegaard, provocations: Spiritual Writings of Kierkegaard, compiled and edited by Charles E Moore, Copyright © 2002, 2014, Published by Plough Publishing House, Walden, New York, Robertsbridge, Elsmore

First Published in 2017

ISBN 978-1-9997338-0-3

Cover design by Catford print Centre

Printed by Catford print Centre, 3 Bellingham Road, Catford, London, SE6 2PN

For Dawn

Gary Lacey

Gary has travelled extensively in the UK and abroad, speaking and teaching on prayer, lifestyle and mission. He is a graduate of The University of Manchester and William Booth College, London.

He has a Master's Degree in Mission, and a Specialist Degree in Celtic Mission and Spirituality.

A Former Salvation Army Officer, Gary now works as a Freelance Writer and Speaker in the UK.

He is married to Dawn, who is a Salvation Army Officer and they are based in the North West of England.

Recommendations

I have always loved Gary's writing, especially his online blog, The Gary Lacey Files. He totally has a gift of making complex subjects so easy to relate to and understand. This book is no different. Dejunk has helped me to admit to myself that I have cluttered up my life with things that are heavy to carry through my life journey. I am busy unburdening that load now. I totally recommend this book, and I am convinced it will bring help to many people.

(Clara Langworthy, New York, USA)

Superb. It had me transfixed! Hearing Gary speak on the platform though, I already knew he was a sharp communicator.

(John Rice, London, UK)

Wow! It had me excited about the future. A beautiful book of hope.

(Anna Durand, Reims, France)

Prescript

Junk.

A word.

A word that is used to describe things we have discarded, and things we no longer need.

Broken stuff.

Out of fashion Stuff.

Things we no longer want.

If this junk is accumulated it begins to clutter up our yards, our garages, our sheds, our workspaces, even the inside of our houses.

Junk takes up space that could be used for more purposeful uses.

The other thing about junk is that can sometimes become dangerous and menacing.

My wife Dawn and I are in the process of packing up our house in London in readiness for a move to Cheshire in the North West of England.

And

We cannot believe the amount of stuff we have collected. Dawn and I consider ourselves minimalists, yet, we have still somehow managed to accumulate a fair amount of junk.

We've found it in our garage. Like an old suitcase and about five big boxes that we haven't managed to unpack from our last move!

We have discovered so much junk that we don't use.

We have had to look each other in the eye and agree a strategy to clear this rubbish.

We agreed to be ruthless!

What we haven't used or don't want we must get rid of it immediately.

Dawn has this habit of finding things we haven't used and deliberating over whether it could be useful or not!

But

This time we must say no to those thoughts and clear out the junk.

Hey

Our lives can become junkyards!

All to easily.

My life did.

My Spiritual life did too.

Some of that Junk was dangerous.

Some of it took up valuable space that I needed, in fact space that God needed.

Hey

I needed to clear this Junk.

In the pages of this book I will talk about how God brought this to my attention. I will also share some of the experiences I have had as I have gone on a journey to unclutter my spiritual life.

It all began on a dark London morning in a City prayer room. When God spoke to me loud and clear.

My relationship with God, and my Church life, had become so stagnant due to the junk that was taking up the space of my being, that I was feeling trapped. There was an ever-decreasing space in my life for God to work in.

To be exact?

There was more of me and less of God.

I had to address this before I lost my faith altogether.

This time I had to look myself in the eye and adopt a strategy.

To be?

Ruthless!

The junk that was getting in the way, and the junk that was of no use to me had to be removed.

Using stories and experiences from my years in ministry, I want to share how I approached this ruthlessness. I also highlight some of the junk that was found in my own life as I have searched the spaces of my very being.

I have only written what God has prompted me to write.

No more, no less.

My hope is that as you read this book, it will set off a chain reaction in your heart to see if there is any junk lying about in your life, especially your spiritual life. Maybe you are struggling with Church, or your relationship with God has become stale, or worse, none existent? Maybe other people are driving you insane and you are having trouble saying no to these people who are demanding and trying?

Well

Maybe it is time to consider uncluttering?

Maybe it is time to consider offloading those things that hold a person back from living a fulfilling life, and a beautiful relationship with God?

Listen

I pray that the words in this book will touch you deeply, even inspire you.

And

I pray that it will prompt you to try and get rid of pointless stuff, like negative attitudes, wrong beliefs about yourself, and struggles you don’t need right now.

I pray it will nudge you towards uncluttering your spiritual life.

So, there will be less of you and more of God.

Catch you later.

Massive blessings.

Room

I watched my wife very closely.

It was a busy morning in the Sanctuary in West London, a Prayer and Mission centre nestled in a busy street in a busy City. There were homeless guys everywhere. Every prayer room was filled with praying people. The café was in full swing, and the buzz was in high velocity mode.

My wife was running around furiously.

She was answering the call of one person, then running for the phone call that had just come in for her, while she has in her mind that she needs to make a coffee for another, while someone else was shouting her to come and pray with them.

She was running around like a blue backsided fly!

Now

She is the most amazing woman.

She loves to please people.

She will always do her best to make sure the needs of others are met.

I felt a jolt of guilt.

I had resigned from this place as a Salvation Army Officer some months earlier. The Prayer Centre we had helped God to build had become so busy that it really needed two leaders to oversee the team we had developed, and the work which had increased tenfold over recent months.

But

Because of my resignation?

Dawn was now in sole charge.

Hey

She does the most incredible job.

She cares for people with a grace and a mercy that can only flow through her straight from the throne room of Heaven.

But

The nature of the beast is that she really was spreading herself too thinly.

I could see it.

The demands on her were great.

Demands not only from the work at the Sanctuary, but also from the administrational demands of a system that some may argue, that is not really suited to serve the mission on the ground.

This meant that she was running every which way but loose. She was trying to be a Pastor, an administrator, a cook, a dish washer, a prayer minister, a wife, a mother and so on and so on.

The result of this was that, as brilliant as she is, she wasn't moving forward as productively as she would have liked.

She would flop down exhausted at home.

She would say to me just how unfulfilled she was feeling.

She was spinning too many plates.

This would have the effect of making her feel like she hadn't achieved anything.

Yet she had.

I have seen her not able to sleep at night because she has been thinking about the plates she is spinning, or the plates she needed to spin the next day. She was dreaming about the people who needed serving and the problems that needed fixing.

Watching her that morning, I began to look at myself.

And

If I am honest?

I am the same.

Rushing here, there, and everywhere, accepting every speaking engagement I was asked to do, saying yes to people because I wanted to please them. I would answer every single text, email or call that came in for me. I would let other people's problems sap me of my focus in a heartbeat.

And

Frankly

The more I carried on like this, the less productive I was.

This also meant that I, just like Dawn, felt unfulfilled and exhausted too.

In fact, I felt like real life was passing me by.

And

Without meaning to?

My relationship with God kept getting pushed further and further back into the hiding places of my life.

This whole approach to life desperately needed to change.

And

The change started with a scripture, as change so often does.

The living word.

A beautiful phrase.

A phrase I take to mean that God speaks to us through his word and invites us to speak with him.

Listen

I was set to pray one morning. I had walked to the prayer room at 5.30am on a dismal London morning. The skies were dishwater grey. The rain was fine and wet. The cold outside as I walked to the Church did nothing to help me to quieten my mind before God in readiness of a conversation with him.

It was 6am when I arrived at the City prayer room.

I felt uncomfortable as I started to pray.

The first thing that happened was my phone bleeped.

A sound that alerted me to the fact that an email had arrived.

Instead of ignoring it, I fired up my phone and got the email up on my screen.

I was perturbed that someone had emailed me at 6am.

Whenever I get a notification out of working hours I always think the worst.

But

On this occasion

It was just a reminder that a parcel was going to be delivered to me at 8.30am that morning.

I switched off my phone and slipped it into the pocket of my faded old blue denim jacket.

I was immediately under pressure to get the prayer done so I could get back home to sign for this package. Otherwise it meant a trip to the Post Office the next day to pick the parcel up from there.

From that moment, I struggled to concentrate.

Other things began to drop into my mind.

All this clutter in my head was dancing around at will.

As this wild dancing was happening in my mind, my eyes caught sight of a single white bedsheet hanging on the prayer room wall. On the white sheet, someone had stencilled a scripture verse in big black and red lettering.

The Scripture was John 3: 30.

"He must become greater; I must become less."

These words cut through the clutter like a cheese-wire cuts through a block of cheese.

The clutter was suddenly replaced by an uncomfortable thought.

How can you become greater God, when I am so busy and my life seems so utterly intense? How?

Then from the shadows of my heart came a whisper that increased to a much louder voice.

The voice spoke out a word I was not familiar with.

"Dejunk."

I thought to myself what does that mean?

My prayer session had begun.

"What do you mean Lord, dejunk?"

I quickly looked the word up in the dictionary. It said something about Dejunk meaning, "To clear, to dispose of unwanted clutter and possessions."

Then God added two more words to the mix.

He said, "Dejunk your life."

The rest of the prayer session was like a movie in high-definition.

As I sat in the quiet of prayer room two on that dismal London morning, The Lord showed me the junk that was seriously affecting my life.

He showed me that this junk emanated out of several things. The inability to say no, the strong internal desire to please people, and the inner drive to avoid conflict at all costs.

These things I saw that morning.

Contrary to the Scripture, "He must become greater, I must become less," I realised that I was greater and God was less.

God spoke those three words again.

"Dejunk your life."

I left the prayer room and headed back into the dark winter morning, I stopped under the yellow glow of a streetlamp. I went over the remit that God had given me that morning.

I was to stop trying to please people all the time. I didn't have to please people I didn't like either, which was another bad habit I had got into. I was to learn to say no. I was to start facing up to conflict in love, and develop a desire to be a peacemaker. I was to start to focus on the essential things and dejunk the unimportant things.

While I had been praying in the prayer room, I had stolen a single white sheet of A4 paper out of the laser jet printer. I began to write on to it the things that really mattered to me. In fact, writing this book is a result of one of the things I wrote down that morning. I also began to write down things that were just junk, things that I was all wrapped up in that really didn't matter.

I had a deep clarity of mind that morning. I was looking through the lens of the Holy Spirit's splendid eyes. It had dawned on me in no uncertain terms that my life had become a complex mess. Endless emails, constant notifications, meetings that were purposeless, endless hours staring into screens, unhealthy relationships with people who really didn't care about me. Wrong beliefs about myself, negative attitudes towards all kinds of things. All this and much more came to the table with startling vision.

I was tired of this crazy life I was leading.

Something needed to shift.

Change was needed.

And

I was truly ready that morning.

From that moment on I began to make some deep changes.

In the subsequent chapters of this book I will share some of that deep change.

Deep change that has helped me to simplify my existence.

Deep change that hurt.

Deep change that helped me to become less, and let God become greater.

Fast

Why have we fasted they say, "And you have not seen it? Why have we humbled ourselves, and you have not noticed? Yet on the day of your fasting, you do as you please and exploit all your workers. Your fasting ends in quarrelling and strife, and in striking each other with wicked fists. You cannot fast as you do today and expect your voice to be heard on high. Is this the kind of fast I have chosen, only a day for people to humble themselves? Is it for only bowing one's head like a reed and for lying in sackcloth and ashes? Is this what you call a fast? A day acceptable to the Lord?

Is this not the kind of fast I have chosen? To loosen the chains of injustice and to untie the cords of the yoke, to set the oppressed free and break every yoke? Is it not to share your food with the hungry and to provide shelter for the poor wanderer-when you see the naked to clothe them and not to turn away from your own flesh and blood? Then your light will break forth like the dawn, and your healing will quickly appear. Then your righteousness will go before you, and the glory of the Lord will be your rear guard. Then you will call, and the Lord will answer, you will cry for help and he will say, "here I am."

(Isaiah 58; 3-9)

Hey

Fasting is not always what we think it is.

Or not just what the Church has largely confined it to.

In short

Hey

It's not just about food.

This scripture puts that theory to bed completely.

This message is a powerful one.

Yeah

God doesn't want the show; he wants the substance.

Wow, there is a wealth of applicable worth in this text that can help us to simplify our lives and create way more space inside of our lives to allow God to work.

The people God is speaking to in this scripture are the Jewish people who had been in exile and were trying to rebuild their lives.

Yet

It seems a lot of these guys were just going through the motions. Performing religious practices that had become purely ritualistic. A good phrase that we use today for this is, 'Doing what we have always done', just for the sake of it.

They were fasting in a ritualistic way by not eating, but doing it because they had always done it, it was a tradition. They were not focussing on God at all.

Then they wondered why God seemed not to be listening to them.

Their relationship with God was really suffering.

This pretty much describes my own life in Church for the first thirty-five years.

Pointless

And

Fruitless!

I had absolutely no relationship with God whatsoever. Yet I looked the part.

I bowed my head when we were praying.

I looked the part in a Salvation Army Uniform complete with ultra-shined Oxford shoes.

I was always there because of pressure from everywhere.

And I had to be there because a good Salvationist was measured on those things.

People used to call it duty.

How I hate that word.

Duty.

Duty is a concept so obscenely warped in the Church that over the decades I know it has finished people off.

And

Hey

It sure nearly finished me off too!

Duty involves doing what we have always done. It can involve practicing religion without the substance of relationship, These Jewish people were practicing religion out of duty.

But

God challenges them, and us today, and all people throughout all generations, to go down a very different pathway other than duty.

This pathway is found by doing less duty and more relationship. It involves discarding the dryness of ritual and picking up a vibrant relationship with God.

I think this scripture teaches us to join God in his revolution in this world.

To bless and save others.

And this means less of us and more of God.

The warped concept of duty often means more of us and less of God.

God invites us to cease doing meaningless tasks and practices, and redirect our focus towards things that really matter. Especially things that matter to God.

He invites us to change.

To realign our spiritual life.

And

To act.

Maybe one of the first steps to dejunking is to take God up on this offer.

Fasting as God says, when done from the heart, and in the context of our relationship with him, is an amazing tool to help us to dejunk.

Isaiah shows us that fasting is not just about going without something so that God will sit up and take notice of us.

Fasting is about change.

Change that deepens our relationship with God.

And

Change that helps us to find peace and joy in life as we pilgrim towards Heaven.

On another morning, on a much sunnier day in London, at the Prayer Centre that Dawn and I planted in the heart of West Ealing, I arrived early to have a cup of hot, black coffee before I started my working day.

I walked through the electric-grey doors into the main café area. The café doesn't officially open until 10am and this was about 8.30am.

I was immediately in a spot of trouble!

Dawn and another staff member were sitting down to their customary quiet time before the madness of the day began.

I disturbed their silent flow by asking a very important question.

Well, I thought so anyway!

The question was

"What is there for breakfast?"

That question was answered not with words, but with a double stern glare that kind of spoke, with no words needed, that I should shut up now!

So

I crept into the kitchen and made myself a toasted teacake and a Coffee.

I went and sat as far away as I could from the silent duo.

I set my steaming coffee down on the silver café table in front of me. On the table was a pile of magazines. I picked the top one up and began to read.

On the first page, was a very interesting article that caught my attention. It was a piece about how to get fit the Catholic way!

The main sub-heading was a question.

“DO YOU WANT TO FAST THIS LENT?

Then underneath was a series of fasting ideas written by Pope Francis in 2015.

Hey

Here they are

Fast from hurting words and say kind words.

Fast from sadness and be filled with gratitude.

Fast from anger and be filled with patience.

Fast from pessimism and be filled with hope.

Fast from worries and have trust in God.

Fast from complaints and contemplate simplicity.

Fast from pressures and be prayerful.

Fast from bitterness and fill your hearts with joy.

Fast from selfishness and be compassionate to others.

Fast from grudges and be reconciled.

Fast from words and be silent.

Hey

I was dumbstruck that morning.

These things fitted in exactly with the schedule of the journey I was now on to simplify my life.

I could see that if my life reflected these words then things would be better.

And

I thought how uncanny it was that these words fitted in with what the prophet Isaiah was writing.

Hey

It's clear.

If life is hectic and you are having trouble distinguishing your backside from your elbow, if the comings and goings of your average day are leaving you feeling unfulfilled and weary. If you are a Christian and your connection with God has felt weak lately.

Then dejunking is required.

Maybe it is time that you should consider a realignment?

Here's a tip.

Get yourself a sheet of blank paper.

Draw a line down the centre.

In one column head it meaningful, in the other column head it meaningless.

Have yourself a quiet moment.

Contemplate all the meaningful things you have in your life. Then write down the meaningless things.

Be as ruthless as you can.

Then sit back and reflect on what you have written.

This is a cool exercise.

If not a vital one.

Because

It is vital to know from the outset of this journey what is and what isn't junk.

Just fire away on your sheet of paper.

Trust that God knows your heart and will show you your junk and where it is hidden.

God challenges us in Isaiah 58 to dejunk meaningless fasting.

Then he implores us to take on the meaningful things of his fight to release people from the chains of injustice.

We can do this.

Think of all the meaningless things that you carry around with you.

I will give you an example to start you thinking.

One of the pieces of junk I had was due to my inability to say no, a subject we will look at more closely later. I would accept every speaking engagement that I was asked to do. Yeah, I love communicating good news to people, but I learned that I need to be more selective in where I choose to speak.

I remember being invited to speak to around a thousand ladies at a conference for a well-known Christian women's movement. When I arrived at the venue for the event, I felt a bit weird being the only guy there apart from a few techie types running the lighting and multimedia. Also, they had given me a subject prior to the event that they wanted me to speak on. It was simply, what does it mean to be a woman in ministry! My talk should have been a quick one really! Consisting of four words, "I have no idea!" I guess I was having difficulty because I'm not female!

It was my desire to speak, and my inability to say no that were a big problem here.

These two things had taken over the fact that someone else, mainly a woman, would have better served the gathered audience.

The fact is I didn't like saying no.

Not being able to say no can be a catalyst to filling our lives with meaningless things.

These meaningless things are just junk.

This junk minimises valuable space, space that could be filled with meaningful and useful things that have quality and purpose, like family, like those dreams we have, like those prayer times we would like, and in fact, an endless list of other meaningful things.

Do you get the picture?

One of the first times that I said no to a meaningless task, gave me a blast of fresh focus, and cleared the way for a new approach to my everyday living.

Five years ago, I was appointed by the Salvation Army to a new role as West London Development Officer. The Salvation Army had been struggling in that part of the City of London for some time. It was my remit to find out why, and to help to bring some change to that situation.

During my orientation period at my new Headquarters, I was told in no uncertain terms that the very least expected of me was to answer every single email that was sent to me that someone else thought required an immediate response.

For the first year of my appointment, every morning, I would trawl through a pile of emails that had landed in my corporate inbox.

Needless to say

It drove me insane.

My inbox was constantly a sad digital collection of meaningless drudgery.

Ninety-eight percent of this junk was just business for business sake.

On one of those cyber trawls into my inbox, I picked up an email from the finance department. Another pointless communication that 'Required' my immediate response.

Incredibly.

I felt the voice of God in my inner self.

The voice simply said, "Don't answer this email." I was

suddenly overwhelmed with an assurance that God was

giving me permission to say no to this email, and

more than that, I was to say no to the other ninety odd

percent of digital drudgery too.

So

I snapped the lid of my old Lenovo X230 ThinkPad shut.

And

I decided there and then, that despite what my so-called superiors demanded, I would simply say no.

From then on, the only emails I would respond to were those that I knew required my direct input.

Anything else?

Deleted.

Then

Inspired by my email revolution

I had this amazing thought.

What if I applied this same principle to the literally hundreds of pointless business meetings and other meetings I am required to attend?

Guys, the amount of meaningless business meetings and other types of meetings I have had to attend I couldn't even begin to count.

Most of those meetings would eat away at your will to live. They were that meaningless.

Sometimes I would be required to drive hundreds of miles for a meeting and then drive home wondering what just happened.

Mostly

And I mean mostly!

They were a waste of valuable time.

So, hey!

Inspired by my email liberation, I said no to a summons to a business day that I was required to attend, but the meeting had no bearing on me, or required my direct input.

There were people who became furious with me.

But.

I simply raised my eyebrows and stood firm!

I just said no.

No way!

Since that occasion, I have only attended meetings that require my direct input.

And

An amazing thing surfaced through this strategic defiance.

Even though people got furious with me, especially leadership, eventually they began to respect me more.

Making these simple adjustments alone has created a mega amount of space and time that I can fill with way more meaningful things.

I am now on a permanent fast from email trawls and meetings!

When you do your list of meaningless things, be brave.

Saying no is OK!

In fact, saying no is vital to a dejunking of your life.

While I was attending one of those meaningless meetings I am writing about, before my rescue and liberation from them, I had been invited to an away day for the National Office of a Christian denomination I won't mention! We were split up into groups to discuss the prayer life of the organisation. A lovely lady started to bemoan the fact that every week there was a weekly prayer meeting that all the staff of this national office were invited to. We are talking about well over One hundred staff members. This lovely lady's flow was cut dead by a senior department head who was also a minister. This person flew into the conversation aggressively and said these words. "Well, what do you expect? We are a business office, neither me nor my department have time to be going to prayers."

A Spiritual Leader saying, "We don't have time to go to prayers?

These were not the most inspiring words I had ever heard!

And

Mark my words.

Absolutely the wrong approach to spiritual leadership.

That kind of attitude smacks of more of us and less of God.

When

As we have seen

The bible requires less of us and more of God.

Probably this office was peddling a lot of meaningless business.

Yet

God requires more relationship.

And

In my experience, More of God means business takes care of itself.

Hey listen.

Finding out what is meaningless and meaningful to you will be a terrific starting point from which to dejunk.

A set of useful information from which you can plan your fast.

Hey

What could you achieve if you downed tools on those pointless tasks that clutter up your life every day?

What could you fill that regained time with?

Just imagine

Time

There is a time for everything, and a season for every activity under the Heavens. A time to be born and a time to die. A time to plant and uproot. A time to kill and a time to heal. A time to tear down and a time to build. A time to weep and a time to laugh. A time to mourn and a time to dance. A time to scatter stones and a time to gather them. A time to embrace and a time to refrain from embracing. A time to search and a time to give up. A time to keep and a time to throw away. A time to tear and a time to mend. A time to be silent and a time to speak. A time to love and a time to hate. A time for war and a time for peace.

(Ecclesiastes 3: 1-8)

Recently I got myself a new watch.

It arrived in a presentation box.

On the inside of the lid of the presentation box was a quote from Thomas Edison.

It said this

"Time is really the only capital a human being has, and the only thing that he cannot afford to waste."

Reading this quote had me thinking.

What do I fill my precious time with? What do I do with it? How much of it do I waste?

Hey, I love the book of Ecclesiastes.

In arguably the most famous part of the whole book is the passage above.

Reading it closely.

You begin to sense just how much of a gift from God that time is.

There is a time for everything.

Yeah

It is capital.

Worth everything in terms of our lives.

It is worth a fortune not in money, but in blessings.

Make no mistake

It is the most valuable gift God gives us, no matter how prolonged or how short our time is, there is an impact to be made.

I remember sitting with a 90-year-old lady in the final days of her life. Time had been long in terms of her life span, but now seemed so short to her. Every system in her body was saying goodbye to life and shutting down one by one. But her mind remained as sharp as a surgeon's scalpel.

She had the most vibrant green eyes set deeply into her dramatically lined face. These eyes caught a hold of my own eyes as I sat holding her weather-beaten hand.

She held my gaze for a long time.

Then

She spoke.

With a forced rasping whisper, she asked me what I most valued in life?

I had to think.

Hard.

I came up with a few things.

God, my wife Dawn, my family, Liverpool Football Club, My puppies Jake and Ruby.

Those green eyes seemed to double in intensity.

Her face suddenly became a picture of wisdom.

And

She was wise for sure.

She spoke these words over me.

"Gary what you should value most is your time. You should fill it with purpose and meaning. Gary, God uses you to touch people's lives, and he will use you more if you value the time that you have been given. It's never too late to start valuing your time."

I was moved to absolute tears.

I knew God was speaking directly to me in that moment.

And

You know what.

This event came to mind as I was writing this, and a thought blazed bright in my mind.

The thought was that time is the most important consideration when we are getting rid of junk. Life is time. Time is space. Space can get cluttered with junk.

I was thinking of the words this amazing Lady had given to me while praying in the vestry before I was about to conduct her funeral.

I was thinking how that for a large part of my life I didn't value time.

There have been large swathes of time that I have just wasted.

And

As you are reading this I guess you may be thinking the same thing?

I wanted to say this right now.

The final words to me from a lady full of the wisdom of God.

It is never too late to change that!

It can happen right now.

A friend of mine was drawing up the inventory I spoke about, the list of meaningful and meaningless things.

She was so frustrated.

And without thinking echoed the opening words of the whole book of Ecclesiastes.

"Everything is meaningless."

She went on to say how she was struggling with her meaningful column, but was not struggling at all with her meaningless column.

She said she had no idea where her priorities lay.

"I can't seem to get my priorities sorted," she cried in vain.

It turned out that there was not enough room on the A4 sheet to write down all her meaningless things, all the junk she was carrying around on her life journey.

But

She mentioned an important thing.

Priorities.

What is that word?

What does it mean?

I remembered as I was thinking about this, about a meeting I had once attended. Yeah you guessed it, a pointless meeting. It was a meeting that required my attendance but had no relevance whatsoever to either me or my ministry.

Someone had invited a speaker.

As soon as I saw this guy I should have known.

He had what seemed like a two-foot forehead. He also had a drastic comb over that adorned the top of his large head. He wore a pristine pinstripe navy blue business suit, with a crisp white shirt and a company tie. He carried a fake croc skin attaché case. And his voice was a bit too posh, so posh that you just knew he was putting it on.

He started speaking about how successful he was.

He spoke about how his company had become successful because of a strategy that he had laid down.

He said he had taught his employees how to prioritise their daily work.

He said he had gotten each employee to write down a list of ten priorities that they would stick to throughout the year.

Fast forward twelve and a half years?

His company has gone bust.

What struck me was the word priorities.

I looked it up.

And

It turns out that the word priorities originates from the word 'prior.' Prior is an ecclesiastical term derived from a Latin word that means 'First thing.'

So

Priorities then could mean First thing?

So how can you have ten first things?

I guess over the years prioritise has come to mean listing things in order of importance.

I'm playing with you a bit here, but I think it is an important point when we consider dejunking our lives.

My guess is that this Company's employees were so busy spending time on their ten priorities, That the one thing that they could do well got lost. They were probably spinning too many plates.

Dejunking requires us to look at the essential thing. One thing that we can do well. Then throw our energy and attention toward that one thing.

For example,

I love writing.

As a minister in a denomination that doesn't understand that not all ministers are talented worship leaders, or gifted speakers, or great administrators, or superb pastors and so on, but expects you to do all these things, my writing often got reduced to a little hobby that I did if I had some time to kill.

Fast forward to today at this hour, I have taken my writing to be an essential addition to my life, as well as something that God has challenged me to take into the world.

In my work, communication is my first thing, my priority.

Hey

What is the first thing, the essential thing that you need to spend a lot more time on?

What junk is stealing your gift of time?

What so called priorities are you wasting your time on?

Hey

I'll give you another example.

When I resigned from my Salvation Army Officership, I took a job with a top London Funeral Director.

I was working as a none-denominational Minister, conducting funerals, and helping to arrange funerals.

I know it sounds a bit deathly, but after the denomination I had just left? It was like finding life for the first time!

Hey

I really loved it.

And

The money was great, the people were caring, the leadership were refreshingly honest and professional.

On top of all of that.

At that time?

It felt like I was making such a difference to people's lives in probably their darkest hour as they had lost loved ones.

But after a year or so of doing this alongside speaking, writing, and helping Dawn when I could, I was starting to spin too many plates myself.

My time was beginning to be filled with too many things, way too much junk, and my quality time was getting less and less.

And

I had been challenged by God to write a book.

When was I going to find time to do that?

One morning.

I felt the Spirit of God whisper directly into my heart.

"Quit your job."

I responded to God, "But Lord, I have bills to pay, how will I live? If I write a book, who will read it?

Again, I heard a gentle whisper.

"Quit your Job. I will take care of you."

Suddenly, fear was taken over by a strange but lovely feeling of liberation.

Right at that moment I was totally in God's hands.

So

I rang my Funeral boss.

There and then.

The conversation went like this.

"Hi Ed."

"Hi Gary"

"Sorry to bother you Ed but I quit."

I won't divulge the response that came back to me, as I would have to write swear words!

But

I quit.

At first, Dawn thought I had gone mad.

But.

She would tell you right now that as we prayed together to launch this new freelance period of my working life, and as we asked God to bless his business through us, she felt a calm reassurance flow into her.

She would tell you right now that since I quit she has not worried for a single minute.

So

Because I had now shifted my paid job out of the way, I won't call it junk because I loved the funeral business, I now found I had bought myself a whole massive batch of time.

And I knew I had to use it well.

By filling it with things that I identified as essential, in fact the one thing I do well, communication.

Amazingly as I work now every day to communicate the love of Jesus to those who would hear, I can honestly testify that God has taken care of me.

I still get asked to conduct funerals, I frequently receive invites to speak, I often write for people, and the money seems to come in from seemingly nowhere.

Just enough to give Dawn and I a beautiful life.

I have also worked hard to furnish my life with times of relaxation, play, and fun.

I have become truly productive.

I count it as a miracle.

When I was spinning too many plates, undertaking way too many tasks at once, I was only mildly productive. Learning to dejunk has helped me to become way more effective.

And

I truly understand what a dying 90-year-old lady said to me that day in a Hospital Ward.

“Value your time and use it well.”

Of course, please don’t put this book down and phone your boss and quit!

Unless you really know you need to!

But

Ask yourself a question.

What is the essential thing that I can do well?

Noise

In 2013, Dawn and I moved to London.

We arrived there fresh from five years developing a Prayer Centre in the Northern City of Durham, and building up a declining congregation in a Village Salvation Army Corps in Sacriston.

Durham is a gorgeous City.

While we were there, we lived out in the hills that surround the quaint little City, in that lovely Village called Sacriston.

It was quiet.

London is very different.

The very first thing that hit us when we arrived in London to the house in Hanwell that would be our home for the next four years, was the noise.

The house was located on a main London thoroughfare, just two miles from the main runways of London Heathrow Airport.

Sirens, traffic, building works, road works, aeroplanes, foot traffic, music, barking dogs, there was every type of noise imaginable!

Pure noise!

It was relentless.

Like Frank Sinatra's assessment of the City of New York, London is also a city that never sleeps.

Hey

Believe me

It is noisy.

It was very difficult at first to switch off.

This constant battle with the noise, ushered stress into our bodies.

My life as a minister up until that point had not been a very positive one. I had been through the mill. My ministry had been tumultuous and noisy. We saw so much victory, but at that moment in time we knew we had been in a battle.

Well-meaning people would say to me that the life of a prophet throughout history does not make a person popular, and that I should just shrug it off and accept some of the abuse that came my way.

But

I neither felt very prophetic, nor like I should accept it.

I had been hurt

Probably too many times.

But

The truth is that I don't fit into denominational Christianity very well. This is mainly because I love Jesus so much, but hate religion so much too.

When I say I hate religion?

I mean its sad dark side.

I totally dislike the actions of denominations that construct a bunch of rules and regulations in an office somewhere, and then put them on all those who are part of that denomination, and throw them at you from every angle because some geezer with a leather chair and a nice big desk thinks that is how people should worship, dress, act, pray, and think.

Hey

I would like to say here that that is my personal view.

And

I would like to recognise that this won't be the case for every Church Leader or Christian who may have had a more positive experience of denominational life.

But for me? All of that was serious noise.

The noise of religion.

So

Here Dawn and I were.

Cast into the middle of the noise of the City of London, carrying the inner noise of the battle to try and survive the outer noise of the Church!

It was in the first few days of arriving in London that I realized I would have to dejunk the religious noise that was by now, at that stage of my ministry fourteen years in, beginning to wear me down to nothing.

In fact, I was depressed.

How did I tackle this?

I resigned!

I will speak more about the resignation and the depression later in the book.

It was the greatest single decision of my entire life next to marrying Dawn!

The noise was too great.

And

I needed to be led beside quiet waters.

Resigning brought me to a safe harbour, and quietened my inner noise.

Not only did I resign

But

I took an indefinite break from all things Church.

This will not be forever.

But

God gave me this time to realign my relationship with Him. A relationship I was so desperate to build up, a relationship I deeply needed.

My life was so full of noise I couldn't fully grasp the hand offered to me by a wonderful saviour.

So, hey.

I took the time.

In those two years, I have discovered way more about God and much more about myself.

It is a bit like when I write, I need a quiet space. Space to think clearly and engage with God effectively, so that I can write words that I believe he would have me write. My writing room is an upper room in an old Church. It is quiet, bare, and away from the noise of the City street. All I have in there is a chair and a table. No distractions whatsoever.

This kind of scenario I also desperately needed in my life.

A quiet space.

Setting Church aside for an indefinite period gave me the quiet space I needed.

Just me and God

The space I had created by listening to, and being obedient to God, was bare and basic, and lacked the noise of religion.

I gained a pure quietness.

Many years ago, I did a Master's degree in Mission, specialising in Celtic Mission and Spirituality.

I wrote my dissertation on the practice of silence.

I discovered then, that silence is mainly a lost experience in the church today.

The Church likes to fill its activities with noise.

For centuries, silence was important, especially throughout the monastic movements.

I studied the differences and the associations between noise and silence. I even experienced some real-time silence in Monasteries, joining Monks in their daily prayer rhythms.

I also learned how to experience silence in the noisiest of places.

To be honest.

All that experience was breathtaking.

And

I had come to a point in my life where I needed to silence the noise and be still before God.

The very first Sunday that I had as a former Salvation Army Officer, was incredible.

I had pretty much attended church from the day I was born.

But

On this day?

I was free of it, for now.

That morning I went for a walk in Osterley Park, close to my home in London. Osterley is one of those rare swathes of Parkland located in the Inner City, that once you are in it, gives you the feeling you are in the countryside. It has beautiful green wooded areas, a country like mansion, a lake, and gorgeous peat-laden pathways.

There under a willow tree looking out across the lake, I read psalm 46:10.

"Be still and know that I am God."

My goodness

The penny dropped straight away.

I was to stop what I was doing, stop what I was experiencing and truly get to know God.

God had placed purpose on this dejunking of the noise I had been living in.

In fact, I knew God was speaking.

“Just stop.”

“Be still.”

“Stop doing, stop worrying, stop surmising, stop day dreaming, stop feeling bad, stop hurting.

Just stop.

I felt the yearning of a God who loves us to the moon and back.

I felt his longing for us to connect with and hear His heartbeat, hear his voice, feel his feelings, experience what he is experiencing. He desperately needs us to hear from him.

And

Believe me

I needed to hear him.

I needed him to cut through the noise of my existence and land his warmth on me.

I know you are reading this and maybe thinking that God is in the noise too.

Of course, he is.

But He asks us to be still

And

Then we will truly get to know Him.

Hey

Our lives can become so full of noise that we struggle to connect with God.

Yeah

My experience of Church has all too often been like that.

For instance

In our services, why do we have to fill that time with relentless music, relentless speaking, announcements, background music, praying out loud and the like.

Just writing this now, I remember going to speak at a so called Mega-Church one Sunday morning. They were filming the service so they were asking the younger, better looking people, to fill the front three rows so it would look better on camera! Can you believe that? There were lighting crews, media crews, worship videos on numerous screens all over the building. It was noisy!

Just before I was about to enter the building ready to speak, I needed the loo! So, I headed off to the nearest lavatory.

Worship music was even being piped into the toilet!

You could not get away from the noise.

You couldn't even go to the loo in silence!

There is just no time to think.

There is just no time to be still.

There is so much noise.

As I have gone around the country teaching, I have sometimes experimented with people by challenging them to be silent.

Even for the briefest of periods.

And

I have learned something I already knew myself

Being still is the most uncomfortable thing for those of us who live life amid the noise.

After one of these experiments, a guy came up to me afterwards and told me that the practice of silence was meant for the medieval era, and suggested that I was living that far back in my Christianity! He went on to finish his mini rant by claiming that I was totally irrelevant and should leave the Church and join a Hippy Commune!

Bring it on baby!

Seriously though, being still, to so many people is hard.

Hey

I am not saying that worship, word, and other noise is not important.

Of course, it is!

But

Just not relentlessly!

Be still and know that I am God.

Listen guys

God doesn't always need a pianist playing soft music in the background, or a brass band parping away with their merry tunes, or an organ whirring, or a guitar strumming.

No

Neither does He always need us to create an atmosphere for him to work in. He is supremely capable of bringing His atmosphere to us.

I will never forget in Sanctuary 21, the Prayer Centre God raised up in the City of Durham, when a lady, who was really struggling with a significant issue in her life, came to Dawn and I for prayer ministry.

She was deeply troubled, and genuinely needed help.

She had come to us for prayer ministry a significant number of times before and, despite our counsel and prayer, she didn't seem to be getting any further ahead.

One afternoon she came for her prayer appointment.

Before any prayer appointment, Dawn and I would pray together first.

As we were praying before this appointment, I had an overwhelming sense that God was speaking. I also had an overwhelming sense that he was asking Dawn and I to step aside that day. He asked us to send this lady to prayer room 3, with no bible, no notebook, no music, absolutely nothing.

It was clear God wanted to minister to this lady directly that morning in the silence.

So

We explained the situation to the lovely lady, making sure she understood this was not Dawn and I ducking out of our responsibility, but God's requisition.

She was cool with that.

So

She headed off to Prayer Room 3 with some trepidation.

Three hours later

She emerged from the Prayer Room looking somewhat radiant!

Her smile was infectious and her cheeks were a kind of ruby-red colour.

By all accounts?

God had changed something in the silence.

And

She had the most unimaginable healing of the emotional strain she was under.

Dawn and I were reminded that day just how able God is.

He chooses you and I to help him to minister His love to people, and to work signs and wonders in the lives of others, but listen, as Dawn and I were so remarkably reminded that morning, it is Him doing the work!

His life changing work!

He heals, He transforms, He restores, He changes things!

And

He does this when we are still before him.

When we cut the noise, and listen to him.

When were you last quiet?

When did you last have some just you and God time?

Hey?

I know it is hard.

Yet

Nevertheless

It is vital.

It is hard, believe me, that's why I suspect the Church doesn't like it anymore.

Because maybe we will be forced to face up to our demons in the quiet, maybe we will be forced to confess things maybe we think are hidden?

Hey

Find yourself a quiet space.

Even if it is the loo! (Not the one in that church mind you, because you will get 'How great is our God' pumped in full blast while you are simply trying to do whatever you do in there!)

Take nothing with you to your quiet space.

And

Then

Simply be still

Know he is God.

Come on.

You've put up with the noise for long enough.

You may have suffered, and not been able to connect much with a saviour who loves you.

Dejunk

Remove the clutter of noise.

Digital

I heard it said somewhere, I can't remember where, that Facebook is bigger than obesity and just as lethal.

Hey

I believe that it is not just Facebook, or Twitter, or any other digital social network platform, that can be lethal, but I believe it is the whole digital life that we so often lead, if not controlled properly, can be utterly lethal.

It can rob time, space, purpose, vision, you name it can steal it from you and can slaughter you at the same time.

Dejunking my life, I knew almost immediately this was one big piece of junk that I had to dispense with.

I was living a life shaped by notifications!

It simply had to be sorted.

Look at 21st century life!

Just look at it!

Of course, there is great value in innovation and technological advancement, and there are obvious advantages to using technology especially in communication.

But

In excess

It is lethal.

Compare life now to the pre-mobile revolution, well those of you who remember that anyway.

It doesn't seem five minutes since I was a young lad running around Liverpool looking for a phone box to call people.

No mobile, no instant access to any kind of information other than what was on Television or Radio.

We wrote things down on paper with a pen!

Life was so simple.

I can remember when I was a mischievous young lad sitting in the house with my mate, and calling the talking clock in the USA just because we could! I remember how we listened in awe as we were connecting with a voice from the other side of the Atlantic!

It seemed utterly awesome!

That's how simple life was!

Nowadays, I talk to colleagues and some of my blog readers in the USA in the blink of an eye, and just consider it normal.

Hey

Communication was very different back then.

I got consumed by the digital revolution the day I was given a Nokia brick phone by my work at that time.

That consummation has grown to the extent that in the present day, I must have a phone, a computer, a tablet, an ebook reader, a digital voice recorder and a digital writing tablet.

I was living my life from my smartphone.

I was hammering the social networks and littering my day with constant emails, tweets and other notifications.

My eyes seemed to be permanently fixed to a screen of some kind.

Even when I managed some down time, I would plug in my earphones and watch a movie, browse the net, listen to music, or do a spot of gaming.

Even when I did graveside ceremonies, weddings, or spoke at church, I would use a tablet computer to jot a few notes down. I would be saying "Earth to earth, ashes to ashes, dust to dust," when a notification would fire up on my screen usually a picture of someone's dog or something!

I can even remember once doing a sermon at a Salvation Army Corps one Sunday morning, at a particularly stagnant Corps, the people there that morning weren't really engaging with the sermon, when a notification appeared on my screen in the top left hand corner, it was one of my nephews asking me if I could make it over to a playing field on the Wirral, which wasn't too far from where I was speaking, and play football for his team, because they were short of players. I suddenly had the desire to play footie, so I stopped what I was saying and said to the congregation that I believed God was asking me to finish the service early today, and just said Amen!

Hey, I wasn't a really a good example of a Salvation Army Officer anyhow!

The fact is.

I was always contactable, always available, even when I wasn't available, or shouldn't have been!

Notifications would hit me any place any time.

The problem with this, is that all of that made me less focussed on what was essential or important in my life.

My concentration levels suffered badly.

It says something when a conversation is easier to have over the digital airways than face to face.

It became so bad that I believed my smartphone was my office.

And

It became even worse than that.

The smartphone became not only my work place, but my playground and my recreational space, when the reality is it is not my workplace, or my play place, or my quiet place.

It got to the point where Dawn and I would be out for a nice meal somewhere, and the moment that we sat down we would reach for our phones and stare at our respective screens until the meal arrived. Then when we arrived home, out would come the tech again!

Our conversational abilities took a nose dive.

We realised with a start that we were hardly talking to each other!

My life began to lack some major things.

Conversation, contact, relaxation, silence, time to think, time to pray, time with my lovely family, and time for myself.

My life was being run by a smartphone.

And

That is junk.

So

The first thing I did was sell my smartphone and replace it with a so-called dumbphone.

This was a major change at the time.

My new phone did not have a camera, it had no internet function, there was no access to the social media platforms.

Just

Calls, texts and reminders.

God did not say give up on technology.

He wanted me to practice self-control.

It is vitally important as I communicate to people, that I have some access to technology, so I still have my computer.

But

I regulate the times I use it.

The first few weeks of my digital detox was murder!

I craved my smartphone badly.

But

After a few weeks?

I noticed that this part of my life was changing.

For the better.

At weekends, I was contactable on the phone, but unavailable on the social networks.

If I sat down for a coffee in a coffee bar somewhere, I had nothing to stare at apart from a book (remember those?) Or I would have a conversation with someone (remember those?) In fact, I would have conversations with people who I normally wouldn't have even seen when my eyes were glued to a screen. I began to appreciate the environment around me, watching people and nature. I even had to use road signs instead of the satellite navigation on my smartphone. Although I have now bought a Sat Nav to help me to find places easier.

But

The biggest thing?

I created a lot more space in which to engage with God.

To pray

To be still

It has brought a new dimension to my life that had got lost in the digital world.

It is kind of exciting to have conversations with people on the phone instead of emailing them.

It also means I can just deal with essential things. The rest of the time is available to me to enjoy stuff that doesn't involve a screen.

To be honest.

This simple adjustment has helped to give me my life back.

A digital detox.

And

Detox isn't too strong a word because in my case, I don't mind admitting I was addicted to technology.

It was lethal.

Lethal because in truth, it had the capacity to destroy my work, my marriage, my relationship with others, and, my relationship with God.

Fast forward to today?

I have removed this piece of Junk from my life and I am managing my digital life much better.

Maybe

Just maybe

This is resonating with someone out there?

Hey

Are you one of those people who say they really can't find time to pray, yet seem to find the time to spend hours on social media or do a spot of shopping online?

Then

Maybe

It is time for you to consider dejunking this piece of junk from your life.

Decision

I was trapped

Trapped by a denominational system

Trapped by religion

Trapped by myself

Trapped by the actions of others.

Totally and utterly trapped.

That's how I felt.

I couldn't move, I couldn't breathe, I felt like I was living outside of my own body.

Something really had to change.

I was heading for a town called oblivion.

My head was all over the place, and I felt like my life was degenerating into just an existence rather than a joyful experience.

This is how I felt for a large part of my time as a Salvation Army Officer.

My life should have been so fulfilling.

Yet it soon became apparent to me that my life as a Minister could only be OK if I towed the party line.

You know?

If I conformed to what some so-called hierarchy said, and didn't challenge anything they said, and totally agreed with them at all costs?

As one very senior church official once said to me, "Gary, if you keep your nose clean, you will go far in this organisation."

I have a very unclean nose!

Towing party lines just for the sake of it just doesn't sit well with me.

Not at all.

I remember being excited to be asked to do some teaching at a conference in Sweden. The headquarters went through the proper channels of inviting me. So, they sent a written request to my National headquarters who then sent the request to my local headquarters.

The request was denied.

The result of this was relayed to me from Sweden.

Those guys couldn't understand at all why they wouldn't allow me to go.

So, I challenged my local leadership personally.

The reason that they gave me?

Was because they wouldn't want to upset all the other ministers, who would wonder why they couldn't go.

Yeah!

This is the worst type of control in action.

And

This is one of the many examples of the stifling effect of a system gone mad.

And

After fifteen years of that kind of restrictive attitude?

I plunged further and further into a darkness that was so horrible that it seriously nearly killed me.

I was well and truly trapped.

I later understood this darkness to be clinical depression.

I will speak about depression later.

I became very indecisive in this period of my life.

So much so, that I was incapable of making a decision of any kind.

Indecisiveness is junk.

It can keep you in the dark places of your life forever if you let it.

All this changed for me on a sunny afternoon in Stratford East London.

I was coming out of the rather industrial looking doors of a six-story red-brick building, close to the Olympic Stadium in London. I had just finished a session with my counsellor.

She was the most pleasant and brilliant lady.

I had been sent to counselling after going through some serious hurt in my ministry that inflicted some serious wounds spiritually and mentally.

The counselling lasted for exactly one year.

In the session, she had given me some unbelievably great advice. Advice that would change the course of my life forever.

She described the denomination I had been so cruelly wounded by, as a tiger in the room.

We had been discussing my indecision. Which was preventing me from tackling the situation head on.

She said that this tiger kept on biting me.

And

Furthermore, instead of getting past the tiger, I kept going back to it for help, but it would just keep on biting me. She showed me that as it kept on biting me it was taking bigger and bigger chunks of my life away from me.

She said, Gary, you cannot keep going back to the tiger for help.

I guess because we lived in a house owned by the denomination, and drove a car supplied by the denomination, and on top of that we had spent any savings we had on getting us through College, then I was fearful of losing all of that. So, I would stay with the tiger, who just kept on biting me.

But

That afternoon

As I strolled out into the heat of a summer afternoon in East London, I had this overwhelming desire to make a decision.

A decision I should have made a long time before.

So

I picked up the phone and dialled the number for my immediate leadership.

And

There and then.

On a City street.

I handed in my resignation.

I wasn't resigning from ministry, I knew that.

But.

I was resigning from the Salvation Army.

And that was that. I called time on my denominational ministry full stop.

But

The reason I tell you this?

Is that it was the fact that I made a clear decision that was important.

And

I learned that clear cut decision making creates space and time.

Decision making is vital to change.

If we are to attempt to dejunk our life, and learn to be more focussed and less distracted, then we must develop the ability to make clean decisions.

A clear yes, or a clear no.

Not what I call, incremental decision making, you know, changing a bit here and there.

No

Deep change.

If I am honest I had known for some time that I needed to quit for my own sanity. But I would come up with incremental change ideas like, If I moved appointment maybe things would get better, or if I go on a massive spending spree maybe I would feel much better.

I would also come up with little defence strategies to try to minimise the hurt, like avoiding Conferences and events to avoid meeting someone or hearing something that would stick yet another dagger in my flesh.

But

None of these incremental changes or defence strategies took the pain away.

It was like just sticking a plaster over a festering wound.

I was procrastinating.

I was effectively staying with the tiger and just let it bite me repeatedly.

Doing these things only made things worse.

Soren Kierkegaard, in his difficult to read, but amazing set of writings called provocations, writes,

"Can there be something in life that has power over us which little by little causes us to forget all that is good? And can this ever happen to anyone who has heard the

call of eternity quite clearly and strongly? If this can ever be then one must look for a cure against it. Praise be to God that such a cure exists- to quietly make a decision. A decision raises us with a shock from the slumber of monotony. A decision breaks the magic spell of custom. A decision breaks the long row of weary thoughts. A decision pronounces its blessing upon even the weakest beginning. Decision is the awakening to the eternal.

Yeah

The cure to something that is eating away at you is to make a decision.

A clear yes, or a clear no.

That kind of decision making leads us into the spaciousness of the eternal. A place where you can breathe again, laugh again, relax again, play again and work again.

This spaciousness gives us the arena in which to connect with a loving God again, and to experience the life force of His Holy Spirit.

This spaciousness also gives us the room to connect with our true destiny and our true purpose.

Being decisive, helps us to thwart the influence of people who fail to take care of you.

This spaciousness gives us the ground to rediscover who we are and who we are meant to be.

Hey

After I had made that clear decision I had to go home.

I was a bit worried when I arrived home to tell Dawn I had resigned. I had not spoken about it beforehand with her, and she had no clue that I was going to do it.

Why would she?

It was a spontaneous decision.

I thought she may want to kill me!

But

Again

She was remarkably calm.

And with that clear-cut decision made, a whole new era opened up before my very eyes.

I was sad it hadn't worked out with the Salvation Army, given that I am a fifth-generation Salvationist. And just as much I was hurt by a few, I was blessed by so many too.

And

I truly want to give thanks for the Salvation Army and pray that it's future ministry is touched and blessed and that it will flourish in the fight. I really do.

Hey

But now I am free.

I feel connected with the eternal again.

It was the decision that made that possible.

Someone maybe reading this right now and find that something is stirring within you. Then I would urge you to consider making a decision on whatever it is that you know needs dealing with. Consider it in the assurance that God will take care of you post-decision. If there is something big or small contaminating or disturbing your life at present, or something is preventing you from realising your dreams and visions? Then make a decision. A clear yes or a clear no.

Dejunk the indecisiveness.

Here is a blog post I wrote back in 2011.

I hope it helps

The countryside is flashing by the semi panoramic window of the trans Pennine express train to Edinburgh. And.

I am easily drawn into a sharp, clarity of thought.

Times are changing for me. A new season dawns.

I have fresh optimism.

Fresh forward vision. Fresh hope.

It feels like I am standing on the precipice of something good.

It feels liberating.

As the beauty of the countryside that adorns the lake district that I watch through the train window plays out its breath-taking scenes, I wallow in the freedom that decision making brings.

It feels like I have been on a roundabout of indecision for such a long time.

But recently I have made a serious life decision that will be revealed in the coming month or so. Indecision is a dreadful thing.

It has battered me, worn me down, worn me out, frustrated me, fed me false convictions, convinced me I am useless, poured guilt into my mind like scalding oil, left me ruing missed opportunities, and virtually immobilised my life. Indecision is a sad thing as far as I can see.

Making a decision is like turning a key to the city of freedom.

So Why do I write this today?

I want to encourage anyone who is on that same cycle of indecision today. Get off the roundabout. Choose freedom.

Choose a new life. Don't let indecision mess with your head any longer.

Make the change.

Take the plunge.

Pack up your old life.

Leave behind those things that you need to get rid of. Walk forward.

And don't look back

No

Hey

I wonder if you have ever found yourself feeling so busy that you feel stretched to the limit? Your work and home life has become a cacophony of busyness and you are convinced it can never change? Yet, even in the busyness you feel like you are not getting very far, and you don't seem to be getting any further?

Yeah?

Huston, we have a problem.

I was stuck in this type of existence. One step forward, two steps back, it was like walking through treacle with rhubarb under your arms.

Listen

The most likely problem that you may have is not being able to say no.

When dejunking our lives, then we must become familiar with the word no.

And

Furthermore?

When we become familiar with it, we need to learn how to use it.

I was the world's worst when it comes to saying no.

And

I have met plenty of others too.

I remember a fellow minister telling me a horrific tale.

This lady, this amazing minister, was wheelchair bound. Her husband, who was not a minister, had secretly booked a dream holiday for her, and had surprised her on her birthday with it. The holiday was going to help this lady to fulfil one of her dreams.

Her dream was to ski in the mountains of Aspen, Colorado.

So

Her husband arranged a holiday with a specialist company that could make this happen.

Excited, she called her headquarters to book the time off officially.

Her request was immediately turned down.

The reason?

Because there was a "business day," that all officers were meant to attend that fell in the week she would have been in Aspen.

Can you imagine the stress that caused this lady and her husband?

She was struggling to say no.

Clearly this is a very sad story.

But

I empathise with her.

I had this reluctance within me to say no.

I can guarantee you that now, in the present day, I would have just said, I'm going. If the trade-off was a trip to the boss's office for a dressing down, then bring it on!

My problem used to be that I just couldn't bring myself to say no.

This dropped me into all kinds of trouble.

I once visited a well-known Theme Park with my wife, my daughter Bailey who was about 11 years old at the time, and her friend Melanie.

Let me tell you right now I hate fun fairs.

I don't mind walking round them, or having a go at some of the sideshows, like shooting pop-up ducks or darts or whatever. I can also just about tolerate the ghost train or some kind of water ride.

But

I absolutely can't go on anything that goes around and around!

It messes with my constitution.

On this day?

Bailey and Melanie were adamant they wanted to go on this particular ride, I can't recall what it was called, but it whizzed around very fast and rose upwards and downwards at the same time.

Melanie and Bailey were imploring me to join the two of them and Dawn on this ride.

I should have said no.

But I couldn't resist their pleading little faces!

So, I climbed onto the ride.

It started.

Within a few seconds I knew I should have said no.

The speed of the ride and the circular motion made me disorientated.

I pleaded for the guy to stop the ride.

Obviously, there was no way he was going to do that.

Bailey and Melanie thought it was so funny they were almost splitting their sides.

When the ride eventually stopped.

I stepped off and couldn't stand properly.

And for the rest of the day?

I spent the time trying not to be sick.

Apparently, I was a vivid shade of green!

That

Was down to me not saying no when I should have.

Another example of my inability to say no was when I was invited to speak at yet another event that I should have said no to!

I was invited to speak to a regional gathering of Senior Church leadership from different denominations.

I was asked to speak about Risk Taking in ministry.

I could tell before I was even introduced that I should have said no.

Most of these guys Idea of risk taking involved little more than moving chairs or asking Mrs Dawkins to step down from the Parish council!

And

I could tell they were ready to slaughter me.

As I finished an impassioned speech about some of the risks I had taken in ministry to attempt to reach the lost and the broken, four people out of the fifty stood up and clapped! The rest had faces like bulldogs chewing a thistle!

After the session, the slaughter started.

Some of the guys who attacked me verbally, performed speeches way more impassioned than mine, and one or two of them used words that I never would have expected senior leadership to use, I just convinced myself that they were Hebrew words!

I spent the next few weeks worrying about what I had said that had stirred them so much, and feeling angry at the ungodly behaviour quite a few of them displayed.

But.

Here is the thing.

I should have said no.

There are certain things that you can never change or speak change into.

And

This was one of those occasions.

Saying no would have saved me two weeks' worth of unnecessary turmoil.

I used to find it so hard to say no. No to absolutely anything if the truth be known.

I would accept invitations to speak at conferences, churches and other events way too easily. I would not ask myself important questions like, Is this event right for me? Am I right for this event? And most importantly I wasn't in the habit of asking God is this right for me?

People would call me up and say, "Gary, I'm not feeling so good, could you stand in for me tomorrow morning and do a funeral?

I would say yes.

People would call me up and say, "Gary, could you do a meeting for me on Sunday morning as I can't be there."

I would say yes.

People would call me up and say, "Gary, Mrs Brown hasn't had a pastoral visit for three days could you pop in and see her?

I would say yes.

Someone would call me up and say, "Gary I need to talk to you right now."

I would drop everything I was doing, and say yes.

All this served to do was create a cauldron of busyness.

I was so busy.

Busy pleasing people.

Busy burning myself out.

Until?

I learned to say no.

A guy I know shared this story with me.

His wife had been very ill with Cancer.

He went to visit his wife in the Hospital where she was being treated.

As he was visiting, his smartphone bleeped out a notification tone.

He read the incoming message immediately.

The message was from his boss at work. The message was his boss asking him to come to work immediately as there was an impromptu meeting happening, a meeting that quite possibly meant a fantastic contract could be tied up ahead of schedule.

He looked at his wife, so ill lying in the hospital bed.

And

He struggled.

He felt the tension.

He knew he really needed to stay with his wife.

Yet

His boss was adamant that he needed him at work right there and right then.

He relented, and left for the meeting.

Later that day he learned his wife had deteriorated somewhat and he needed to get back to the hospital.

Listen

The inability to say no always has consequences.

Consequences either for us or for someone else.

This story had a happy ending as this guy's wife eventually made a remarkable recovery, and is now in a lengthy remission.

But

When he was sharing this story with me, he acknowledged some important things.

He acknowledged that he had subscribed to the way of the world that we live in, a world which wears busyness as a badge of honour. A world that says if you are busy then you are successful. If you are busy, then you are productive.

I myself was caught up in this thinking.

But the above story shows that it's not all about busyness and productivity.

In fact, it tells a very different story.

That if we want to show success that involves hurting others, even family, then we can expect failure.

The only antidote to the busyness of life is to say no.

I had to say no to something in the last few years that was hard to say no to.

And

It turned out to be the catalyst to a new dawning for me. A dawning that saw me start to understand and use the word no to great effect.

My immediate leader had looked after my resignation from the Salvation Army with great care.

She made it easy and smooth.

One afternoon, post-resignation, she came to check that Dawn was OK.

In this meeting, I was there too, she started to say to Dawn that it would be great now because Gary could help her with the work at Ealing, and that he could even become part of the leadership team.

Of course, she was being kind and thoughtful towards Dawn.

But

I had to say no.

Not that I didn't want to help Dawn, but by this time God had already spoken to me about setting the Church aside for the foreseeable future.

I was to concentrate on building a stronger relationship with him.

So

I said no!

As hard as that was, it was so liberating.

By saying no, it released a whole amount of space for me in which to carry out what God required of me at that time.

I had lost some sparkle in my relationship with God. I had lost something of the connection I needed with the Holy Spirit. All the religion of Church, the rules, the regulations, the structures, had served to reduce my relationship to, 'Hanging by a thread,' status.

The first Sunday morning that I didn't attend Church because of the sabbatical God had installed, I felt so free.

As I said earlier, I went to a local inner London Country park for a walk with my puppies, Ruby and Jake.

I had an amazing time that first morning.

It felt like the first morning of the rest of my life.

I walked.

I prayed.

I wrote in my journal.

I found I could reconnect with the Spirit of God that morning.

The reason was that I had created some much needed space by removing the clutter of church. All this was made possible by saying no.

I had such an encounter with God that morning, an encounter that had eluded me amidst the busyness of Church.

This encounter breathed new life and new resolve into my being.

I get utterly concerned when I hear other leaders in Church say that cringe worthy phrase, usually in the guise of a question, "Where are you getting fed?" I so dislike that terminology. Do these people think Church is the only place where spiritual food is served? Do they not think God is capable of speaking directly to people? Do they think God, the ultimate teacher, confines his life lessons to Church services?

I don't think so.

Obviously, teaching, preaching, and other Church activity is deeply important when delivered in an engaging way, but it is not the be all and end all.

Oh my.

Is it no wonder Jesus needed to be alone on occasions?

It has been amazing during my time without Church getting in the way, just how close Me and God have become.

I have learned to depend on him more, to rely on him more, I've learned how gracious he is, how loving he is and how beautiful he is.

I know that I will need to return to the Church when God says the time is right, but I will go back much stronger and ready for the fight again.

I think this verse in the message bible sums up what I have been experiencing perfectly. I have learned the unforced rhythms of grace.

In fact

Saying no can open the way to experience the unforced rhythms of grace.

I leave you in this chapter with that verse for reflection.

Are you tired? Worn out? Burned out on religion? Come to me. Get away with me and you'll recover your life. I'll show you how to take a real rest. Walk with me and work with me-watch how I do it. Learn the unforced rhythms of grace. I won't lay anything heavy, or ill-fitting on you. Keep company with me and you'll learn to live freely and lightly.

Rest

Someone responded to a blog post I wrote recently.

This post challenged people to take a real rest.

The person who responded is an amazing lady and a great Christian leader.

She shared with me how her life had become such a mess, and that she felt that she had nowhere to turn. Her ministry had become impossible to carry out.

She was suffering badly with stress.

In short

She was burned out.

Her words to me told some important things.

She said, "I know I need a rest, but I just can't see what that rest will look like. I am so busy, and I worry that if I do take a rest from Ministry then my boys may not go to church, and I worry about their walk with God."

Another friend of mine told me that he too didn't know how to rest well. And he said that when he thought of all the people he knew and loved, they didn't know how to rest well either.

This got me thinking about rest.

It is safe to say that I also struggled to take a rest.

Why is this?

Especially in the light of that scriptural invitation from Jesus himself, imploring us to take a rest with him.

He also says that he will "Show us how to take a real rest."

I think as I prayed and asked God to show me how to take a real rest, I have learned a few things.

I was burned out on religion.

Religion had worn me down to nothing.

I want to share with you what I have learned about rest.

As I share, keep in mind that there is much more that we will learn about rest on our Christian journey than what I share with you here.

But

Before we look at what rest is, we need to understand that we get tired.

Tiredness, scientifically speaking is a normal function of brain that informs us that we need to take a rest and replenish our energy levels.

It is inbuilt into our anatomical systems for a reason.

It is a kind of warning alert.

But

Hey

How often do we ignore that warning?

How often do we just carry on regardless?

Some people even wear tiredness as a badge of honour. They think that tiredness is something to be admired, and marks them out as special.

I honestly thought this myself.

This the indestructible approach to life, where a person is convinced he or she is indestructible.

Hey

Listen, superman or wonder woman or whoever you believe you are, no-one is indestructible.

No-one is safe from the grip of tiredness, tiredness can take a hold of a person and totally overwhelm them.

Hey

A short and succinct prophetic word has just dropped into my head while writing, so I drop it in here.

If you are tired?

"Stop now!"

The lady I mentioned at the start of this chapter is a prime example of how tiredness gets it's claws into a person.

She is so obviously tired and burned out on religion.

But

She is letting other thoughts interfere with her need to stop.

What are you tired of?

Religion? Work? A situation that has been a constant thorn in your side? Has another person been wearing you down? Are you tired of being broke? Is that boss at work doing your head in?

Hey

Come on?

Be honest with yourself.

What is driving you towards total wipe-out?

This lady needs a total rest; she is so tired. But I suspect she is having a tough time allowing the fact that she needs a rest drop from her head to her heart.

Hey

And

That creates an open invitation to fear and doubt and other nasties to walk right on in to your life. They worm their way in between the lines and blur the whole picture.

Oh yeah.

Fear, doubt, uncertainty and insecurity like to mess with the body, mind and spirit of a person.

They like to encourage you to bypass the warning sign of tiredness.

This lovely lady has a genuine concern that her boys may suffer if she has a break from Church. That is fear and doubt walking into her life without authorisation.

They breeze in like they own the place.

Hey

Here is something the word of God says about how to counteract this.

Cast all your anxiety on Him because he cares for you. (1 Peter 5:7)

Yeah

Listen

God will take care of you if you would only keep your eyes fixed on him.

And

More than that

He will take care of all those things around you too.

Work, finance, family, whatever it may be God will take care of it all if you will go to him and give him your everything.

Listen

Harbouring doubt, fear, worry, and other insecurities only serves to make you even more tired and wearier. Mark my words, they also have the capacity to rob you of Joy. They suck the energy out of a person and draw them further and further into the whirlpool of burn out.

Hey

Say no to fear.

When I was going through my resignation process, I had a major wobble.

An incident that nearly harmed me and pulled me back down into the darkness I was just coming out of.

I had a visit from my boss again.

She was checking with me that I had made the right decision.

Just before she left she made this remark.

"You had better be sure about your resignation because there is no going back, the Salvation Army will not have you back as an officer."

It is a good job Jesus doesn't close doors as easily as that. His arms are always open.

But

I guess the Church has its reasons for slamming doors shut.

The reason I am telling you that is this.

That closing remark helped me to open a door for fear and doubt to creep in.

And they walked into my life and tried to make themselves at home.

Negative thoughts started to flood in as I sat in the quiet just after she had left. "Have I done the right thing? How will I live? Am I putting immense pressure on Dawn?"

These were the doubts flowing in to my head.

The fear and doubt were so strong that I almost called my boss up there and then to cancel my resignation.

This was despite the fact that I strongly felt the Lord giving me permission to leave.

This was despite the fact that I knew I had got past the tiger in the room and was preventing it from biting me ever again.

I desperately needed to quit and stop being bitten by the tiger, but I was considering going back to the tiger for help.

But

This time?

I didn't allow fear and doubt to settle.

With all the strength I could muster, I said no.

I needed to put the tiger in a cage

And

I believe this is where we must understand that burn out comes from a desire to be a special person, a person who is tireless, a person with immense stamina.

Hey

No one is that person.

Who are we trying to impress?

Quite often we are trying to make an impression on people we don't even like!

Listen

Having this indestructible nature?

It makes you tired.

Hey

It really does and tiredness renders us ineffective no matter how much stamina we think we have.

It was a good decision to usher fear and doubt out of my own life.

Insecurity and all that it brings with it is junk.

Once I had cleared out that junk

Once I had won that battle, the journey of rebuilding my shattered life began.

And

The first thing God laid on my heart as I started a fresh new chapter in my life, was that I needed to learn to rest.

So

He said this very profound thing.

"Gary, get a dog!"

This was something quite unnatural to me.

I had never in my life had a dog.

I must confess I didn't really like them either.

But

Trying to be obedient.

Dawn and I travelled out on the M25 on a cold Sunday morning, and picked up an 8-week old puppy. A cross between a Pug and a Border Terrier.

His name is Jake.

He is two and a half now.

And

I can honestly say

This little fella has helped to change my heart completely.

And he has helped me to discover new avenues of rest and relaxation too.

Then

Inspired by Jake

We got another dog.

A pedigree Pug.

Her name is Ruby.

Oh dear.

I have fell hopelessly in love with both!

Everytime I walk in the house regardless of what kind of day I have had, there they are at the door with their tails wagging, Jake's like a helicopter blade, Ruby's like windscreen wiper on a slow setting! They are so pleased to see me.

When I walk them, I see things I would have missed, I have met people I wouldn't have met.

It has been a total success.

These two little dogs, have been a big part of me recovering my life.

Here is the weird thing.

This is what happens when the Lord shows us how to have a real rest. Do not be surprised if God lays seemingly mad things at your door.

God asking me to take a rest from Church was strange enough, but get a dog?

But God always has reasoning behind these things.

And the thing is when we are burned out and tired, the tendency is to run away from God.

As one guy pointed out to me in no uncertain terms by telling me that I was blasphemous, disrespectful and sacrilegious for leaving Officership, and that I was running away from God.

In reality?

I was running towards Him.

Right into His precious arms.

Christianity needs space to cultivate. I knew I was burned out on religion, and desperately needed quality time with God. Father and son time. I had to trust the Holy Spirit for my healing and listen to Him as He directed my steps. I needed to stand face to face with God without the Church getting in the way. It was incredibly liberating to dispense of those pressures. God and me, we were free to just talk to each other. My sleep came easier. I found that I had developed a wrong way of looking at the needs of the world around me. I was looking at it through the Churches eyes, but now found that I was looking at it through Heavens eyes.

Listen

A real rest involves a restorative process that enabled me to rebuild and put back together a life that had been smashed apart from the relentless attacks of religion.

Allow God to restore you.

Allow God to help you to rediscover your purpose.

Here is a word for you.

"Tired warrior.

You are tired. So very tired, and you feel devoid of any imagination? You feel like you have nowhere else to turn? You cannot carry on doing those things that are just sapping the life from you. Lay down the heavy burdens that you are carrying, lay them at the foot of my cross. You don't have to carry them any longer. Listen to me child, close your ears to the constant calling of the world. Open your ears to my voice. I am gently calling you to another way. A way that is restful and peaceful. Step away from the pressure. Step away from the noise.

Come with me."

Energy

Hey

Many of the people I have ministered to, when asked what they believe the purpose of rest is, really can't answer that question without straining hard.

Rest

The purpose of it is to re-energize the body, mind and soul.

A battery can't go on forever.

It must get a recharge.

It is the same for us human beings.

We run out of energy if we don't recharge.

Energy depletes as we spend it.

And

To be effective, productive, and content human beings, then we must recharge our batteries.

And

The recharge mechanism God has given us?

Rest.

Hey

A big part of dejunking involves replenishing our energy levels properly and sensibly.

This guy came to me once for ministry. He was a former professional footballer who had just recovered from a big heart attack that almost took his life away from him. He had not long undergone major open-heart surgery. When he came to see me, he had already started undergoing the mother of all lifestyle changes. Chatting to him, I asked him what caused his illness? He said, "That is easy Gaz, I ran myself into the ground, almost literally!" He went on to tell me that he had set up a chain of dry cleaners, plus a hotel business since retiring from football. He said that he had felt that he just had to throw everything at this business to increase its success rate. He told me that he had to work 16 hours a day to maintain this.

Until.

He keeled over with severe chest pain while mowing the lawn one Sunday morning.

His battery had run dangerously low.

Speaking to him that day helped me to focus on my dejunking more readily.

Because I also asked him another very important question.

“Now you are changing your lifestyle, what do you think the most important change that you have to make is?

He replied.

“I need to rest.”

I am learning that I must replenish my energy levels.

I am building a proper rest schedule into my everyday living and I have to stick to it, in between if I get tired, I stop.”

His life had been so busy and so full on that he simply ran out of energy. In this case, it manifested itself as a heart attack.

Lack of energy can have all kinds of manifestations and consequences, physically, mentally and spiritually.

And

When we ignore the warning that is tiredness, they will appear in some form.

The excuses that we make, and believe me I have made these excuses, are dangerous in their seemingly innocent form.

Excuses like, “People can’t do without us, the Company can’t do without me, the Church can’t do without me, I am tired but I’ll have to go.”

These excuses that favour carrying on regardless, lead us to the land of burnout, meltdown or death.

And

I am sure none of us want to go down that pathway.

So

Take rest seriously.

Learn the unforced rhythms of grace.

Get your sleep.

Know when to stop.

Know your limits.

Are you feeling weary?

Carrying junk makes you tired.

So here is a second warning.

Dejunking means getting rid of the desire to keep going relentlessly when you are tired.

Get rest now.

This will replenish your energy levels.

It will make you fitter and sharper and more productive.

And

It will breathe fresh life into your spirit. Fresh energy and fresh effectiveness.

Prayer

And pray in the Spirit on all occasions with all kinds of prayers and requests. With this in mind, be alert and always keep on praying for the Lord's people.

(Ephesians 6:18)

Prayer has so many aspects and angles.

It can change you.

It can change a situation.

It can Change others.

Ultimately it can change a Nation.

Back in 2002 I was walking through Victoria Train Station in Central London.

I saw something beautiful.

It was the first time I ever saw the electric connection between prayer and mission.

In a dark, dirty corner of the Station, I saw a young girl sitting with her back resting on the wall.

Her hair was matted and dishevelled, her clothes were inadequate for the biting cold of a Winters evening in London.

Pain was written across her countenance.

She was homeless.

You could see the sadness and the weariness etched into her eyes.

I watched as another girl, also very young but much healthier, go up to this young homeless girl and kneel beside her.

She whispered something into the young homeless girl's ear, the downtrodden girl nodded as if to give her permission for something.

Then she placed her hands on her shoulders and began to pray for her.

I watched in awe as I saw the tears streaming down the young homeless girl's face.

And

I swear I saw the face of Jesus in that moment.

I saw them hug and then stand up together and disappear into the rush hour crowds in Victoria.

She was probably taking her for some food and drink.

And

I knew then.

Prayer changes things.

Sometimes powerfully, sometimes gently.

It not only changes things in the lives of others.

But in our own lives too.

Prayer is the lifeblood of our relationship with Jesus.

I fell in love with prayer the moment I came to Jesus and gave my life to him.

Listen.

I had never prayed up until that moment.

Not in any meaningful way anyway.

That sounds so crazy considering I have been attending Church pretty much since I was born.

Hey

I would look like I was praying.

In Church, I would bow my head with the best of them. When I was a child I would rattle out gentle Jesus meek and mild before I went to bed to pacify my parents, I would look almost angelic when joining in the Lord's Prayer at Church.

Hey

I could look like a saint.

I was a very good actor.

But.

They were just hollow words.

I may as well have been praying to a wall.

I should mention here that for the first thirty-five years of my life, I was a Salvationist, but had absolutely no relationship with God whatsoever.

I looked like I was praying but there was nothing behind the words at all.

All that changed the moment I encountered a magnificent Saviour.

It is no wonder that for a large part of my ministry I have travelled across Europe speaking and teaching on Prayer.

It has truly become second nature to me.

And I have learned on my journey that without a vibrant and healthy prayer life? Then a relationship with Jesus is impossible.

I worked that one out for myself within days of becoming a Christian.

I was overwhelmed with the fact that I could just chat to God wherever and whenever I wanted to.

Prayer must be the central element in getting rid of any junk from our lives.

Why?

Because it is God who does the work, he guides, helps and administers the dejunk.

And

As we have already been reminded.

We must become less and God must become more.

So, let's talk about prayer simply.

Let's look at its basics.

Here is the most basic thing about prayer.

We need to talk to God and we also need to listen to Him.

Put simply

This is a normal conversation.

Like you would have with anyone.

But

This type of conversation is the most important conversation you will ever have because it is an eternal conversation and it is the fulcrum of our relationship with God.

Obviously, there are many aspects and types of prayer, but for now we are talking about personal, relational prayer.

Would you please forgive me if this chapter sounds like a 'Read with mother' session or a Sunday school class, but listen, one thing I have noticed when travelling around to many different Churches, massive, medium or small, is the fact that all too often prayer is the least understood practice in Christian life.

And

If you really think about that?

That is mad!

I know there are many reasons for this.

But

It is safe to say that without constant conversation with God? Then last man out of the Church hand the keys in on your way out!

Without prayer, you can forget dejunking your life.

When Dawn and I were Salvation Army Officers in the North East of England, I met a guy called Gary.

Gary is a down to earth North-Eastern guy who calls a spade a spade.

The first time I met him he said to me, "Don't talk to me about God because I don't really believe that stuff.

About a year later, after Gary would meet with me every week for a coffee to talk about whatever we felt like talking about, especially religion and Christianity, he gave his heart to the Lord.

About a month after he had become a Christian he came to me one time and said, "Gaz, will you show me how to pray?"

So, I arranged to meet him in Durham at our Prayer Centre, Sanctuary 21.

We got ourselves a hot black coffee each and headed for prayer room 2.

I started talking to him about prayer from the standpoint of the prayer that Jesus taught us to pray.

We spent a bit of time talking and praying the Lord's prayer.

The conversation switched around to looking at ways we can talk to God and how to listen for his voice.

Then Gary said something that made me wonder who was teaching who that night!

He said “I guess I will just have to trust the answer God gives me. If I hear anything from him, I will trust him. I guess that is what faith is, is that right Gaz?”

Here was a new Christian working out what Faith is, this early on in his walk with God.

I was dumbfounded.

And

For me

I learned something that has stuck with me.

Faith and trust are the vital ingredients in any prayer life.

Trusting God, even if his answers aren’t what we hoped for.

Then

He asked me something even more profound.

“Gaz, why do people only seem to pray in prayer meetings?

Hey

I started to shift in my seat because this is a question that I have asked many times.

Let me tell you that God liberated me from prayer meetings at an early stage in my own Christian Journey.

Not that prayer meetings are bad, or wrong, or shouldn't take place. Nor does it mean prayer times in services should be abolished!

But

Like Gary, I couldn't get my head around why conversation with God seemed to be confined to these set timetables.

I remember being ushered into a side room in a Church one Sunday morning. I had been asked to speak in the morning service and I had arrived early consequently catching the pre-service prayer meeting that apparently had been running weekly for around forty years.

So

I joined them.

Six people including me.

The congregation expected that morning was around Three hundred.

It is safe to say that this prayer meeting had probably seen better days.

We sat in a bland circle in a bland, magnolia painted room, on metallic chairs that could shine the toughest of trousers.

We bowed our heads.

The leader said a short prayer.

Then, like a game of pass the parcel we went around the circle saying a prayer each.

I kind of lost the will to live.

It was like undergoing a general anaesthetic.

Getting sleepier and sleepier.

I almost floated off into oblivion.

And

This was before I had to preach a sermon to Three hundred people.

Hey

The service wasn't much livelier either.

After the prayer meeting the guy who seemed like he was the leader of this group came to me almost apologetically saying the usual things people say when they are embarrassed about the meeting. He said, "We were short today, we usually get eight people but a few people are away." I asked him what he thought of the meeting. He said, "If we didn't do it then there would be virtually no prayer in the church."

I admired his will to see prayer happen, but I saw a deeper problem.

I saw that these guys were confining prayer to this gathering.

I wanted to shake this church out of its slumber.

I felt like hammering home some massively good news.

News that reads, "Jesus is alive."

Yeah.

That means he is available without limits.

The early Celtic Christians who had mostly converted from Paganism to Christianity were brilliant at prayer.

They kept it simple.

They kept it real.

They prayed about anything and everything to do with their lives.

If they boiled some water, they prayed about it, if they were going on a journey, they prayed about it, if they were about to crack open a hazelnut or whatever they did, then they would pray about it.

They developed a simple but effective lifestyle of prayer.

They understood this.

That God invites us into His life and we must reciprocate the offer.

This is what is so liberating about prayer. You do not have to wait until the next general anaesthetic, sorry I mean prayer meeting, to have a conversation with God. You can develop a lifestyle of prayer and allow God into every aspect of your life.

I tried to teach Gary about a lifestyle of prayer and how that can affect both us and others.

A few weeks after our conversation in Sanctuary 21, Gary shared with me that every morning he would drive the same route to his place of work.

Every time he drove up a certain hill on that route, he drove past an old guy who had walking sticks and seemed to struggle up this hill.

Gary started to pray for him.

He said he felt that God was telling him to stop and offer this guy a lift.

So

True to his word.

Gary trusted what God was saying, and stopped for this guy one morning.

The guy was so grateful.

And then Gary continued to do this day after day.

This is the sheer raw power of a lifestyle of prayer.

God shouldn't be restricted to prayer meetings or prayer times in Church. Learning to bring God into every aspect of our own lives, and I mean every aspect, the good parts and the bad parts, has a major impact on who we are as a person. It also has an effect on others as the above story shows.

Hey

If you have a boring, or even worse than that, a none-existent prayer life?

Get rid of it.

It is junk.

Open your heart to a vibrant new lifestyle of prayer that changes us and changes others.

Don't put up with the mediocrity of a prayer life that happens only in set timetables.

Hey

He must become greater we must become less.

It makes so much sense to dejunk our lives of spiritual dryness.

Start bringing God into everything.

Not everybody believes that prayer is vital.

I know that sounds daft.

But I know it to be the truth.

I had been invited to speak at a prayer conference in North Wales.

It was a big gathering which was being followed by a 24/7 week of prayer.

I had been asked to speak a kind of motivational talk on the power of prayer, with the aim to get people excited about the week that was to follow.

There were a lot of people in my session, around two thousand, and as the session concluded there was hardly any room to move, as the organisers had set about ten different hospitality stations along the back of the auditorium so that people could get refreshments between and after sessions.

I was literally gagging for a cup of tea, and was holding on to the hope that there would be biscuits too.

I was standing in one of the queues and people were kindly thanking me for my talk and giving me some great encouragement, when out of the corner of my eye I saw a guy right at the stage end of the auditorium, and he seemed to be heading straight for me.

His face had “I am angry” written all over it.

I tried to turn my gaze away from him because I was so determined not to be caught by an angry person, because I really needed my tea and biscuits!

But

Right enough!

He came straight for me.

He said in a vicious tone of voice, "Can I have a word with you!"

I led him away from the queue to a quieter corner of the arena.

He said, "Those words you have just spoken from the stage, can you honestly say that you believe prayer works?"

I replied calmly, "Yeah I do, I wouldn't have said them if I didn't mean them."

"Well," he retorted angrily, "I believe it is all rubbish. I know for a fact that prayer doesn't help anybody."

"Anyway," He continued. "Does the Salvation Army have a scientific department that can prove prayer works?"

I replied, with tongue in cheek, "I don't think so, no!"

He went on further, "Tell me this, if you were placed into a Russian Roulette situation and had a gun to your head, and you didn't know whether the next shot would kill you or not, would you pray then?

"Look mate, that is one time I would definitely be praying," I replied confidently.

He looked me straight in the eye and said, "Well I wouldn't, prayer doesn't help anybody."

By this time, I was beginning to wonder why this guy was at a prayer conference, and I was starting to be convinced he had just come in off the street to cause a bit of trouble, so I asked him.

"Do you go to Church?"

"Oh yes," he replied, "I've been an elder in my church for fifty years."

Fifty years!

Fifty years this guy has been a part of the leadership team at his church.

And he doesn't believe in prayer?

Of course, I was flabbergasted.

But.

Sadly, as I have travelled around teaching on the subject of prayer, I have come across this before, albeit not quite so in your face as this guy was, but I've seen it.

That is just unbelief.

But

I have also met Christians who are desperate to have a vibrant living relationship with God yet struggle with prayer.

Hey.

If we want to dejunk the scourge of spiritual apathy, then we have set to work on our prayer life.

Starting with just you and God.

Abandon the confines that we so often set on prayer, and discover the prayer life that God is just waiting for you to have.

And be blessed.

Word

I met John in Liverpool at the turn of the millennium.

His story inspires me even today.

It will do forever.

He told me about his years as a narcotics addict in Anfield, Liverpool, a very tough area that required a person living there to be acutely street wise.

He told me how he had lived in a flat with his grandmother. His life and addiction had become so bad, he had become almost solely confined to the apartment, only opening the door for his drug suppliers. He said to me that he was probably only weeks away from death.

Then

One afternoon his grandmother died.

This left John alone to struggle with his addiction.

A few days later he was cleaning out his grandmother's things. In her big old wooden wardrobe, right at the bottom of it, under a pile of old newspapers, was a Bible. A large, leather bound King James Version that was tattered and frayed and had seen better days. John scooped it out from under the newspapers and set it down on the kitchen table.

Then.

Something unimaginable happened.

John says, he opened it to the first chapter of Genesis.

He started to read.

And read.

And

Read.

He kept on reading for two or three, maybe even four or five days and nights, he didn't know how long.

He read chapter after chapter.

In fact

He read from Genesis to Revelation in one sitting.

And.

Then.

Something miraculous took place.

He had begun to read the Bible every day.

He had never been to Church and never spoken about God with any Christian ever.

Every night before he went to bed, he had developed a ritual.

He would shoot up, in other words inject heroin into his arm, and then he would say the Lord's Prayer which he had learned direct from the scripture. He said it because, as he told me, it was a prayer Jesus had taught us to pray. Then he would go to sleep.

Then one night, he had just performed this nightly ritual, he shot up, and then began to say the Lord's prayer when he began to feel very strange. Just as he started to say the Lord's prayer, he experienced what drug addicts call a whitey. In other words, he had just said "Our Father" when he was sick everywhere.

Then the next night the same thing happened.

He shot up, started to say the Lord's prayer, and there it was again, he was sick again.

Then on the third night the same thing happened again, this time though, he said "I was wise to it this time and made sure I had a plastic bag ready!"

As he thought about this, he thought to himself, "This must be this Holy Spirit that is mentioned in the Bible."

He thought, "Maybe he is trying to contact to me."

He told me he just opened the Bible and read something about losing your life to gain life.

Then an incredible thought came to him.

"He must be telling me to lose this life of drug taking."

And.

Right there and then.

In a lonely flat in Anfield, Liverpool, his 16-year addiction stopped.

Fast forward to today.

John now touches the lives of many addicts as he shares his story with them, supplying them with the hope of a saviour.

Now, those of you reading this who work with drug addiction, will no doubt know that it just doesn't normally happen like this.

This was a miracle of epic proportions, and a miracle that only the Spirit of God can do.

And

When I think of John's story, it speaks to me in many ways.

One way it speaks to me, is about Scripture.

Now, when I write these next couple of sentences please understand that again, I will not be recommending that people give up studying the Bible, if that's what floats your dinghy, nor will I be aggravating Theologians, who's opinions are just that, opinions, but I will be showing you that if we want to dejunk our lives and learn to hear from God, then we have to let the word of God be just that, the living word.

The living word means that he can speak to us through Scripture, no matter how many times Theologically challenged people say things like, "You can't just open the bible and read what it says, you have to know the context etc. etc. Listen the truth is, God can do anything he needs to through scripture because his word is alive and speaks in infinitely different ways to different people and different situations. Look at what happened to John as he just opened the bible! It's fulfilling and interesting to know the contexts and the settings and the Theological arguments presented by clever people about the Bible, but listen, it isn't everything.

And.

John's story is living, breathing truth, that God can speak to the furthest person away from him, without any Scriptural or Theological training full stop.

That is exactly what the living word does!

He saved john.

Literally from death, through His word.

So

Hey.

Here is the thing.

To dejunk all that difficulty we sometimes have trying to understand Scripture? The Spirit of God implores me to write this statement.

Let the living word of God speak into your life unhindered!

In other words,

Make sure you read scripture and listen to God in it.

Not just study.

I ministered recently to a well-known Theologian who has written many books on the subject, and taught at some of the worlds most revered Spiritual Universities and Seminary's. A very talented and learned man, and a good guy too.

In tears, he admitted to me, and more importantly, before God, that he had so much head knowledge, that the truth that Jesus loved him, and the fact that he could have a relationship with him, had become obscured from view. His constant inner battles with Theology had clouded his ability to walk with Jesus every day.

It was breathtaking as we knelt together before the cross of Jesus, and he let the wonder of God cut through the Theology and hit him in the heart.

The clouds that surrounded him cleared.

It changed this guy's life forever.

One of the things he purposefully changed straight away, and I mean the day after our encounter, was that he started to do an ancient practice, practiced by Monastics for century's even to this day as part of their daily offices, called Lectio Divina.

And.

I thought it would be great as a part of our dejunking, to just give a simple explanation of Lectio Divina for you guys to try.

Believe me.

Lectio allows the bible to become exactly what God intends it to be.

The living word.

Making scripture come alive.

Seriously alive.

There is much written about Lectio, and loads of diverse ways in which to interpret it, and it may be wise to seek some of these out, and adapt it to you and your life.

But

Here and now?

I am just going to give you a very basic taste and a simple explanation of how to do it, so you can maybe build on it and adapt it to your personality and needs.

First it is vital to understand the purpose of Lectio Divina.

It does not treat scripture as texts to be studied, but as the living word.

It simply is to allow the Holy Spirit to speak to you through the word of God.

There are four movements or stages of Lectio, and one leads into the other as you start your session.

1. Lectio: which means read
2. Meditatio: which means meditate.
3. Oratorio: which means pray.
4. Contemplation: which means Contemplate.

Find yourself a quiet spot.

You're only going to need half an hour or so.

Choose a passage of scripture. It doesn't matter how you choose it. Even if you just open the bible and read something from the page, or systematically read from the start, or choose verses that are your favourites, or use a daily devotional as a guide, it really doesn't matter. I started by going through the Psalms, that for me was a great starting point.

Then read that passage very slowly about three or four times. Let the words sink in.

Then meditate on what you have read. Have a think about it. The Spirit of God will lead you to think about a certain word or a whole phrase that will be personal and meaningful to you right there and then.

Then pray about what you are thinking about.

Finally, just rest in God's embrace, be silent in his presence.

The word of God will come alive to you by reading scripture this way. Doing this daily will allow his word to become part of your life without the pressure of always understanding the technicalities of theological thinking.

In other words, this is vital for everyone, intellectual or not so intellectual. The bible is for everyone. God would be so mad if his word becomes a thing only for the super-intelligent.

To be honest?

God really wants to speak to us.

And.

It is vital we hear him through His beautiful word.

Tears

The day I became a Christian there were tears. Believe me.

I cried the shame out.

I cried the guilt out.

I cried joyfully.

And

I learned a lesson.

The lesson is

That tears are important in making a person whole.

I believe that the touch of God is almost always marked by tears. When we let God into our lives the reaction is so often to cry. I have seen it happen not only in myself but to thousands of people that I have had the honour of ministering to over the years.

Tears come with surrender.

Working for so long amongst gang members and homeless people as I have done over the past fifteen years in Liverpool, Durham and London, I've seen how often these people are so afraid of tears. They see it as a sign of softness. In their hard lives, fighting for survival means that they don't want to be seen as weak. But It's not just the people who have the hardest fight.

It's all of us.

We try to become resistant people. Resistant specially to change and fear of the unknown. We so often want to cling on to the familiar.

Dejunking means change.

And.

We may feel resistant.

But

Don't be surprised that when we surrender to the changes God is asking us to make, that tears will happen.

My Dad died of cancer a good few years back now. I never had a good relationship with him.

In fact, our relationship was so fractured that I hardly spoke to him, or him me, for many years. He had done some things that had hurt my mum, my family and myself badly. Some of my family members dealt with it differently, but me? I couldn't even look at him without it turning my stomach, as I had seen and experienced some of the pain he had inflicted on us, especially my beautiful Mum.

Yet

In his final hours when death was imminent?

I felt I had to lay that to rest for my own sake and his.

I rushed to his house and asked the lady he lived with to let me have some time alone with him. I went upstairs to his bedroom. I looked at the frail, dying old man lying in the bed before me, helpless and motionless.

I will never know if he could hear me, but I am trusting God that he could, I spoke some words from the depths of my own heart. Words to the effect that I forgave him for all the torment and pain he had caused, and that I loved him as my father, even though he had hurt me so badly.

And

I forgave him and meant it.

As I was speaking the tears came from nowhere.

Tears that I cannot describe.

Big, clear and hot.

But I know that every tear drop that ran down my face that day, carried relief, love and healing.

These tears ushered in a new era for me.

I couldn't have let my own Father go to the grave without him knowing his son loved him regardless. How on earth could I have stood before gatherings of people and speak about forgiveness when I couldn't forgive my own flesh and blood?

Those tears brought change.

Those tears removed the clutter of a whole mess of unforgiveness that only served to hurt us both.

And

I share that with you, as hard as it is to write that intimate and personal glimpse into my life, I believe it will help to describe what God is trying to say to us all the time, that removing the clutter of the messes we make, especially unforgiveness, will create the space needed for more of God to flow into our hearts.

Way more of God

I believe God wants me to make this clear.

Tears play a vital role in uncluttering and dejunking our messy lives.

Don't try to resist.

Let them come.

Let them stream down your face. Let them mark an encounter with the great healer.

Silence

There is a saying.

Silence is golden.

And

It really can be.

But

It can be tough too.

I wrote my Master's degree on silence.

My Degree didn't really matter to me that much, it was always more about the fact that I enjoy reading, studying and writing so much that it is a pleasure more than a chore.

I was more thrilled with some of the lessons I learned when totally looking in to the forgotten practice of silence.

My journey with silence started at an Abbey in Derbyshire. I went on a silent retreat as part of my study. I had to be silent, and I mean silent, for three days.

Oh dear.

It was probably the toughest thing I've ever had to do in my life.

Switching off my motor mouth was especially tough.

But it wasn't just the fact that I wasn't able to talk.

I had to surrender my phone and my computer.

That was a tough goodbye believe me.

The room I was staying in was completely bare except for a toilet cubicle, a shower, a desk, a desk lamp, a chair, and a bed that looked like something that had been brought to the room from a stable.

The room was stripped of anything that can distract you.

I was stripped of everything that could have distracted me.

I felt very lost for a while.

The first day, the first night, and half of the following day, were murderous.

I struggled to settle down, I struggled not to be bored silly, and I struggled to connect with God at any level.

All I could think of in my head was, "I have so much to do, I need to do this and I need to that, and I can't wait until this senseless retreat comes to an end."

I craved my phone that keeps me connected to the world.

I craved the latest Liverpool FC news! I craved conversation, especially to tell people just how numbing this whole experience was.

But

Then

After a day and a half

Everything changed

I mean I went from total unsettledness, to a pure connection with God.

Unbelievable clarity.

Unbelievable peace.

Some Monastic types call this period I went through for the first few days, "The chattering monkeys." Where thoughts fly around in your head like hundreds of screaming monkeys swinging from tree to tree. So much so you cannot settle.

Maybe this is why the practice of silence has faded away from the Church over the centuries. To the point now where we are scared stiff of it.

When I started to receive clarity on that three-day retreat, I realised a quite scary thing.

I was frightened to be alone with myself!

I was worried that I may have to face my demons in the solitude.

And

So

The chattering monkeys were trying to prevent me from facing up to some stuff I really needed to face up to.

But.

Considering that God says, "Be still and know that I am God," in the light of that verse straight from scripture, I began to wonder if that is partly why we are so keen to play background music in church for everything, or make noise, or talk all the time, or sing hundreds of songs and spout off endless sermons. As I said earlier, some churches are now even playing background music in the toilet!

Is it because?

We fear what we may have to face in the silence?

Is it because we feel we are a bit unworthy to be alone with God?

Totally alone?

Psalm 39: 2-3 Sums up the struggle we have with silence.

"I was silent and still; I held my peace to no avail; my distress grew worse; my heart became hot within me.

While I mused, the fire burned, then I spoke with my tongue.

This Psalmist guy was having a bout of the chattering monkeys!

I acknowledge before my readers here, that silence is hard.

But

Silence is golden too.

And it is essential in the process of dejunking.

We need to face up to some the stuff that we need to get rid of out of our lives. Especially the stuff that makes us greater and God lesser.

In that afternoon on my retreat when the chattering monkeys stopped their incessant chatter, and I found myself stripped of all my worldly things and I was alone with God.

A massive piece of junk came to my mind.

A few weeks before the silent retreat, I had overheard someone at a conference I was speaking at criticising my talk from a session I had delivered. They said, "His speaking is too simple. It's alright for illiterate people but for intellectuals it is baby talk."

Yeah.

Those were a fellow Ministers exact words.

Those words stuck like mud to my heart.

So much so.

I lost my confidence in the pulpit a bit.

Everytime I spoke I wondered if I was spouting off baby talk.

Everytime I prepared for a talk, I started to study like mad to come up with some fancy Theology that would feed the intellectuals among us.

Which?

Wasn't really me.

So, my speaking started getting a bit confusing. Well, to me anyway, so goodness knows what the congregations thought! I'd struggled with this for some months. I had been hurt by people's words and the damage was done.

But.

I had swept it under the carpet, I had pushed it deep down into my very being, and didn't want to face it.

Subconsciously I thought it best to just live with the wound.

That afternoon in the silence I had no choice but to face it.

And I heard Gods voice, or saw it more specifically.

I picked up an old tattered book with yellow pages that had once been white. I can't recall what the book was called, or even what it was about, but I do recall the opening sentence of Chapter one.

"Speak the truth, because the truth will set people free. But make sure you speak it with simplicity lest the world won't understand."

And

The clarity began to roll in like the dawn, changing night to day.

I knew God had always called me to preach to the needy and to those who desperately needed a saviour, not really those who were intellectually glorious. I knew that Jesus had spoken in parables not out of text book, and had changed the world forever.

And in that moment as I faced up to this situation.

I knew I had to speak truth simply.

In the silence, in that moment I was able to remove the junk of the belief that I should speak at a more intellectual level to the masses, and replace it with the truth that God had gifted me to speak simply.

It was a classic dejunking.

It's funny because just before I sat to write this segment today I got into my writing room early, and decided to have an hour's silence.

In that silence, I was having an issue with thinking my chapters weren't very long. So much so I grabbed a load of old books off the bookcase and started to count the words.

I heard the Spirit of God say.

"Put the books down. Write what I tell you. If the chapter is only two words long, if I've spoken them, so be it."

Again, I was able to allow the Spirit of God more space in which to create whatever he needs to say and speak through me, whether I like it or not!

Silence gives us the opportunity to hear God. It creates space to see what is going on in our lives.

If you want to dejunk and make yourself less and God greater, then build in some silence into your day.

Work through the chattering monkeys.

Make space to think, and to see inside yourself.

See what junk lies around in your life and take steps to remove it.

Attitude

My seven-year-old granddaughter has a little T- shirt.

On it is written one word.

Attitude!

And

It suits her just fine!

I love her so much

Especially because of her attitude.

She takes no messing.

She is a tough little girl

And

Adorable, all at the same time!

And she is a funny little character.

But

She has an attitude alright!

Attitudes vary of course among all people. You see the calm ones, you see the changeable ones, and you see the completely wild ones, and many variants in between.

I want to be daring straight away and suggest something.

Attitude is a choice.

You ain't born with a bad attitude!

How you decide to tackle life head on is a choice.

You could tackle it positively, or you could tackle it negatively.

I know a guy who makes me laugh without fail.

He is the most negative person probably in the history of time.

The other day he launched in to this big-time spiel about how people who paint graffiti on walls should be given a life sentence in prison. He moans about everything, criticises everyone, and lambasts anything to do with any kind of establishment.

He is extremely miserable.

His attitude is a top-notch production line of negativity.

I feel sorry for him, but can't help liking him immensely. I love nothing more than to see him kick off!

He doesn't know it, but he is hilarious when he is angry.

Here's one of the things the Bible says about attitude.

Do all things without grumbling or questioning, that you may be blameless and innocent, children of God without blemish in the midst of a crooked and twisted generation, among whom you shine as lights in the world. (Philippians 2:14-15)

This guy I am talking about?

He's a minister.

He really should be a shining light?

But

Sadly

His attitude helps him to be not even a dull flicker.

The day he commenced his ministry at his current church, he had two hundred plus people in the congregation at his welcome service.

He even moaned about that.

"Too big," he would say.

Today?

He has four people.

In fact, only two people most of the time because the other two work shifts.

He's been there for three years.

Two hundred people to four in three years?

That must be some kind of record!

He came to me to talk through about why his congregation had so dramatically fell apart.

As he rattled off a tirade of miserable remarks about the people who had left, some to go to other churches, some who he had put off church for life, and knew it!

I saw clearly one of the problems.

It was this.

Negativity spreads.

This guy's attitude was so negative, so defeatist, so beaten, so extreme, that he had undoubtedly communicated this to the people he was supposed to be caring for, and it caught on like a nasty infection killing people's aspirations, hopes and dreams along the way.

So, one by one, family by family, they left.

I asked him in a very kind way, what was his attitude towards his ministry?

He said immediately and without thought, "It would be alright if it wasn't for people."

So

I asked him a question for my own clarification.

"So, let me get this straight, you would like to minister to no-one?"

He set a slight smirk on his face and said, “That would be nice.”

The only answer I could give him was this.

“Well, your well on the way to achieving that goal pal!”

He looked up at me with a worried look in his eye.

I think a moment of lucidity came over him, and he realised what he had just said.

Here is the thing about this.

Our attitudes not only affect our own lives, they have an impact on others too. They can infect others badly. Family members, colleagues at work, friends.

About seventeen years back, Dawn and I did something that we will never do again.

And

When I tell you this, many of you will relate to what I am saying!

We went for a two-week holiday to Florida in the USA with fifteen family members and friends!

I can honestly say I could never do that again?

Yeah?

Comprende?

Anyone else been there?

It began at the airport in the USA.

We had touched down at midnight. It was raining, the person who had organised it had left the address of the Villa we were staying at back in the UK. The only information we had was that the house was in Kissimmee and was painted pink on the outside with the statue of a flamenco in the front garden. We collected our hire cars and headed down international drive towards Kissimmee, to look for a pink house with a flamenco.

Can you imagine?

The tension was palpable. We were trying to drive in a convoy, as we didn't even know what part of Kissimmee the villa was in. If you have ever driven a car in America then you will know it's not like the UK. There were cars coming at us from everywhere.

Unbelievably, miraculously even, after about four hours of searching in the middle of the night, we eventually found a pink house with a flamenco in the garden. We tried the key, and thankfully it was the right house!

It was now about four o'clock in the morning and people were tired. The tension started right there and then.

And

It continued throughout the two weeks, mostly over stupid stuff like, where we would eat, or what part of Disney World we would visit, or who is driving the cars, or what places we would visit, or what times we should set off, things like that.

Oh, it was not fun at all.

And

People's attitudes suffered.

Mostly because everyone wanted to assume responsibility.

Everyone wanted to be king.

Hands up if you have been there?

And this is an important thing to understand about attitude.

Negativity and poor attitudes stem from our desire to control situations. When you are in an intense group such as a family holiday, or with friends, then the trouble is everyone wants to be in control.

In the end

There was some major falling out.

I wonder if you have heard that saying?

He or She needs an attitude bypass?

Well it's true.

And

Dejunking very often requires a shift in attitude.

A bypass even!

I knew I needed this as I began my own process of dejunking my life.

I needed major attitude bypass surgery.

One of the first things I did was to admit to myself that I had become a little negative about things.

Yeah, I had reasons, I had been hurt badly by people in my own denomination, but I knew I couldn't let this drive me under forever. My attitude had become a bit sour, and admitting that to myself meant that I was able to realise that I had to change this.

The thing was that I was getting stuck in a sinking sand of negativity. And in many ways, although it wasn't nice, I was getting more and more comfortable with negativity as I sank further and deeper into the mud.

It's a bit like how the old circus used to train elephants. They would chain an elephant to a tree, and the elephant would struggle to break free for about a month. After this, the elephant stopped struggling and just stood there. This is when they took the chain off. In effect, the elephant could have bolted at this point, but he didn't,

he was trained to stand by the post. He had got si(
struggling and just got comfortable with where he stood.

This was me. I was free to bolt away from the bad attitude I had developed, but had struggled so much I had nearly given up. Even though I could have been free? I chose to stay where I was.

Yet

When I recognised this, I took immediate action to free myself of this.

I changed my attitude.

I chose to do so.

I purposefully set out to stop thinking negatively.

I focussed on the positive things that lay ahead for me. I chose to set my heart on God, and cast all my anxieties on him.

And

I chose to look positively on everything.

I even adopted a kind of open and close door policy.

One thing I had always struggled with was when doors shut on me. I mean, when opportunities faded or disappeared, when dreams were dashed, when things didn't turn out the way I wanted them too, I kind of crashed.

And

I could hardly ever get up from those things and try again.

To give you an example.

I was offered a book launch for this book that was a fantastic opportunity to get it off the ground. It turned out that the date that was offered to me wasn't possible because I was booked somewhere else. They didn't have another date. The negative thoughts I have suffered with on occasion, came flying towards me. Thoughts like, "You may as well give up on this project, it's never going to happen."

Or

"Just bin the book, no-one will read it anyway!

But

This time?

And instead of thinking that this door had shut on me, a new idea to have several book promotions around the UK surfaced, opening another door before me.

This simple illustration is an example of an attitude change.

Negative to positive

And it is important that this takes place in the dejunking of our lives.

And as we go into our lives on a daily basis, we need to apply the principle of turning negative into positive to everything we do.

The other important thing is to ask yourself who is running your life? Who is King? Who is on the throne?

In my experience, it has to be God in control. I literally had to dethrone myself in the dejunking process and allow God to do what he does insanely brilliantly, lead my life.

It's so breathtakingly beautiful not to have to be in control.

To allow God to be in charge.

When we are in control?

Carnage can turn up in a flash.

When God is in control, things are massively different.

Are you tired of negativity?

Do you feel like dejunking it?

Then why not let God be King.

Thin Place

Talking earlier about the ancient Celts, I was reminded about a concept of their early worship that would be good to talk about here. It will undoubtedly spark some thinking about finding a quiet place, not just inside yourself, but an actual geographical location that will help you to feel closer to God.

I don't want to give a theological basis and outline of this concept, because there has been so much excellent stuff written about the concept of thin place.

Just for understanding purposes, a thin place was an actual geographical place where the people who lived in the iron age, and in the medieval era, believed you could visit and experience the spiritual world much easier. This could be a beach or a shrine, or a tree, whatever and wherever.

In other words, there were places special to them that it felt like there was only a thin veil between the natural and the spiritual world.

A place where you could easily engage with God.

A place where a person felt at home with his spirituality.

Thin places are personal to you.

Thin places are your choice.

And

In the times we live in now, thin places are as relevant and real as they were back then.

Many people have re-discovered this thinking and have that special place, or number of places they can go to get up close and personal with God.

For me one of those places is Jandia, on the Island of Fuerteventura in the Canary Islands.

A rugged coastline with pure white sand and a vibrant, turquoise sea that is adorned with pure white foam that is produced from the rolling waves that come in from the African coast, and is washed with the highly-polished glint of the sun as it's rays touch the sea.

It is a complete paradise.

You can walk for miles on Jandia beach and not see another single person.

The dramatic rock features stand like pieces of glittering steel set in a pure white sand, and it all aids the feeling of closeness to God.

There

In that gorgeous place, I have sat so many times and just felt the touch of God on my life like nowhere else.

I remember one year I had a big decision to make about leaving my former career and giving my life to full time ministry.

Back home in the UK I had struggled and battled a bit too long with these decisions.

There were many big decisions to be made, "What will it be like to uproot our girls and ourselves to go to college in London to train for ministry? What would we do with our house that we owned, do we sell it? Do we rent it out? What about the sheer drop in salary that was going to take place? Would we need to take a car to London, if not, what shall we do with our two cars? Would I really want to be a minister? Is it actually about what I want?"

These were the kind of big questions that were running about our minds at that time.

I needed place to think and be totally in tune with Gods heart.

Jandia provided the quiet and the thinness that was required, and for whatever reason I seemed to able to have a clarity there.

It was in Jandia, one unbelievably bright morning, under a pure blue sky and a blazing early morning sun, that I was just sitting on a rock looking out to sea, watching the fierce Atlantic waves crash onto the beach, that I was overcome with the Spirit of God and experienced a hushed voice telling me that everything would be taken care of.

And now, as I look back? He did take care of everything, and continues to do so.

I could dispense with my negative thoughts and doubts that day.

I dejunked them.

When we dejunk, it is nice to have those places we can escape to where it seems that God is easily reachable.

I've found many places that range from cathedrals to coffee shops.

Something to consider is where are the places that you like to escape too?

Is it the beach, a caravan, a country, the countryside, a City?

Maybe you know already where your thin place is?

Maybe you don't?

There is a beautiful world out there waiting to be discovered.

Maybe it's time you paid your thin place a visit?

Have you got some things to think through that you would need God's guidance on?

And you need space?

Find your thin place.

Others

Dejunking our own lives can have a massive effect on how we ourselves go about the mission of letting the world around us know about the fantastic news of the Gospel.

Earlier we considered dejunking our bad attitudes.

How we act towards others is vitally important if we are to be effective Christians.

A few years back I was in the middle of considering a question that could only be answered by God.

We had been asked to plant a new prayer Centre in a UK City, and I, as the vision carrier needed to hear from God whether this was the right thing.

And

If this was his plan.

I had heard a lot about this City, and had just completed a month-long street walk, a kind of reconnaissance of the place, observing and learning about its daily life, so I could get a better handle on what needs lay in its streets.

One of the things I kept hearing as I met different people and tried to learn all I could from them, was that this City didn't need another Prayer Centre, as it had the Cathedral, and this is where people went to pray.

And

This was true in part.

But

I needed to see that for myself.

So

I decided to start my working day, every day for about a year, in the City's Cathedral and pray there, to experience it, to watch others pray, and see what God had to say about that.

One morning I was praying in the Cathedral. Taking in the fantastic architecture and the quiet spaciousness of the ancient building.

As far as I could see, there was no one else in there at all.

I was completely alone.

At the door of the Cathedral there is a sign saying please switch your mobile phones off.

I had missed the sign that morning and had left my phone switched on by accident. I was sitting right at the front of the great ancient building, and had just started to pray when my ringtone, set on full volume, started to sound. I desperately tried to find my phone in my pocket, but it took a little while as I fumbled about in a panic.

Once I had found it I began to frantically try and switch it off.

But before I could stop the ringing, a short, plump lady in a purple cloak, appeared from nowhere!

She came from behind one of the large stone pillars that stand in the Church.

I remember thinking she looked like a big wine gum, and she had the look of a deeply angry person.

"Did you not read the sign," she said in a very authorative tone of voice. "You can't use your phone in here," she continued.

"I'm awfully sorry," I replied meekly.

"I don't want an apology, just leave immediately," she said, she was getting really heated now.

"But I'm praying." I protested calmly.

"Go now," she said with blistering authority.

So, I picked up my bag and my phone, and made my way quickly out of the cathedral into the streets of the stirring City.

I did manage a, "Bless you madam," on the way out, which made her round face almost as purple as her robe!

I walked straight from the Cathedral down to a coffee shop called the Coffee House, which happens to be another one of my thin places. The owners, Peter and Margaret, an amazing couple who aren't Christians, were just setting the tables up for the day ahead. Peter must have thought I looked a bit downtrodden, because he asked, "What's up with you man? I replied, "I must be the only minister ever to be kicked out of the Cathedral." Followed by the rest of the story including the bit about the wine gum! He laughed and said sit down man." He then gave me a free cappuccino and a muffin and said "Hey, well we love ya lad."

As I sat and sipped my coffee

A serious thought in my mind wouldn't go away.

It was this.

I was being shown more acceptance and love from the none-Christian community that morning, than I had been shown by the very community that should have been the open arms of Jesus.

It not only gave me the answer from God that I had been waiting for, that we were to build a house of prayer in that City, but it also made me think about how I act towards others, especially those in need of a Saviour.

I could have been anybody in that Cathedral that morning.

In fact, I was anybody!

I could have needed help, but I was ushered out into the street as if I had committed a crime.

God doesn't really care whether a phone goes off or not in a Church.

He really doesn't.

But

I needed the heads up from God that day, that I have to treat everyone I meet with compassion, love and acceptance.

Otherwise how will people see the compassionate heart of Jesus in our communities?

And.

In my dejunking.

I felt that I truly wanted to eradicate anything that stands in the way of people knowing Jesus through me.

I always want to be the open arms of Jesus to others.

I can't change the Church, and frankly don't need that battle anyway.

but

I see so often Churches that are resistant to the public.

I know that sounds awful, and the Church would deny that strongly, but sadly all too often it is true.

Yeah, I can't change how the Church is

But

I can change how I treat others.

God can change me.

And

We must take responsibility for the inside of ourselves.

Then we will be able to reach others.

So

Our attitude towards others must be in line with Gods attitude.

One of love and sincerity.

One of authentic concern for the welfare of others, spiritually, mentally, physically.

Anything other than that, no matter which way we look at it, is just junk.

The world is desperate for a Saviour.

The world needs you.

Depression

Depression.

What a hideous illness.

Strength sapping.

Stifling.

And

Totally Immobilising.

Those of you who have had depression, or have it now, will know right now what I am talking about.

Its horrific in every sense.

I've had it.

Been through it.

But I have been healed.

I struggled with it for around five years that I know of.

I'm not a medical expert on this subject, so I don't want to go into the medical reasons for depression here and now in this book.

But.

I do want to share my experience.

I began to look at depression as junk.

Because that what it began to feel like to me.

Like I was carrying a whole heap of heavy junk.

But believe me, I do not want to belittle anybody by saying it's easy to just get rid of the junk of depression.

Let's establish that right now.

It is the hardest piece of junk ever to step away from.

This type of junk, depression, can be a killer.

And

I mean it when I say killer.

Out of the hundreds of funerals I have conducted as a minister.

I know for sure that ten of the deceased who I have laid to rest have died as a direct result of depression.

I recently did the funeral of a young girl who had Jumped into the River Thames, and had died as a result of that, even though people had tried to save her. I had to sit with her parents in their front room and try to comfort them. They hadn't realised just how much her depression had spread into her being.

So

Yeah

It can be that serious.

My own depression came from, as I have mentioned, a series of horrible attacks from Leadership in the Church. The very place where love and tolerance should be woven into its fabric.

I can only try and describe how the depression felt every day.

It felt like I had a massive block of steel in my head that physically made my head feel like it was strained to its limit every day.

I felt like I had a weight on either shoulder, pushing me downwards. I sometimes would be walking along a street and feel like the pavement was drawing me down into it.

I couldn't find happiness ever.

I made mountains out of the smallest molehills.

I couldn't stand to see people flourish it made me jealous.

I didn't want to go anywhere, I didn't want to mix with anyone, I found it hard to love anyone, I didn't love myself at all.

I struggled to breathe sometimes.

I woke up with the worst headaches you could possibly think of.

I had a fair few panic attacks.

I became defensive when I was speaking on stage, defensive of myself because I literally thought everybody hated me and no one could possibly like me.

It was a nightmare.

A living nightmare.

For five years, I lived with two faces.

One the public saw.

The other one my wife saw.

I could act well in public most of the time.

But at home is where the real manifestations of my illness could be seen.

I was miserable and had to force myself to do things in the house.

But for three of those years I refused to even think I had depression. Dawn would say to me, "You need to see a doctor," (Mind you she still says that!) I would say, "No chance, I can cope."

Until one day.

I properly hit rock bottom.

I had never ever experienced feeling suicidal for real, and I still don't believe I could ever do that, and I'm reluctant to say I was suicidal, but on this rock bottom day? The thought did cross my mind.

That shook me to the very core.

And

It awakened my senses.

That day I came to the cross.

I knelt down and said to God.

"Here I am God. I am admitting I have depression of some sort here. Help me God please just help me.

As I waited for his answer, I can say that it is one of only two times I believe I've actually heard the voice of God for real.

When I say for real, I mean audibly in the room.

He said something I wasn't expecting.

And

I wasn't sure I liked his answer, and I guess those among you who don't believe Doctors can really help depression wouldn't like this answer either.

He said.

"Go to the Doctors, now!"

Now, I want to just state here for the record, that one thing that I have learned as I minister to many people, who ask for healing of all kinds of illnesses and injuries including depression, I believe God heals. I have seen him heal the most serious of illness in a heartbeat. How he heals is up to him. You may know people who have been instantly healed from depression and I truly believe God does this. Sometimes healing comes through other avenues. I choose to let God decide how healing comes.

God is God.

I guess on this day I didn't have any choice, God directed me to go to the Doctors.

I didn't want the world to know I was suffering. I just wanted to hide it.

But.

Just like Dawn had been telling me

Even God was telling me to go to the Doctors now.

So, I went.

I want to say here and now, that this was the best thing I ever did.

And.

Before I carry on, I want to say that admitting that you have a problem is the first step that you take in the opposite direction to that pathway that leads to oblivion, and leads you towards healing and recovery.

So, if you have the junk that comes with, or causes depression, and you know reading this chapter that this is the case.

Then

Put this book down and make an appointment right now.

I was put immediately onto medication and sent to counselling.

This simple medical plan, along with the prayers of people who love me, helped me to turn this thing around.

I have to say here and now too.

That not only did I, at this point, admit it to God and too myself, I started to admit it to family and friends.

This helped them, because coupled with the medical care, it allowed the prayer to be more informed as they prayed specifically for me, and specifically for my healing.

Once this was in motion.

Depression didn't stand much chance of surviving.

It took a couple of years.

Counselling was something I would often say I didn't really believe in.

But.

I can't begin to tell you how a year-long weekly visit to my counsellor's office in East London helped me to pull myself together.

Just talking.

Was healing.

But.

The skill and dedication of my professional counsellor, especially her skill in directing the talking, was gentle and supportive. She led me gently and expertly to speak out the pain I had.

And

I believe God was at the centre of that work.

The pain wasn't just from a five-year period, I found it went right back to my childhood.

A bad relationship with my father had seen to the fact that I had struggled throughout the years.

She teased out the root of my illness, and I was able to communicate this to those praying for me, so they had more specific information to go on.

I was able to communicate these things to Dawn too, who is the most reliable and loving person I have ever known, and stood by me through the toughest of times.

I stuck to the medication.

I stuck to the advice I was being given by the Doctor.

And

I stuck with the counselling.

I kept on believing in the prayers of others.

I have now been weaned off the medication and I stand now healed and restored.

I feel whole again and ready for the fight again.

So

Hey

I wondered why God wanted me to write this here, but as I am writing, I get it.

There will be people who are reading this and the tears are flowing now?

Not because of what I have written

But rather

Because you recognise you need help yeah?

Here is a plan.

Admit it right now, that is the first thing.

Go to God.

Go to the Doctor.

Follow every bit of advice and instruction you get to the letter.

Tell others

Ask them to pray.

I know it isn't easy.

It will never be straightforward.

But you should dejunk it.

Otherwise what else can you do?

You cannot live with this forever.

And.

You, without help, are on a constant track to possible oblivion.

You don't want that.

God doesn't want that.

Your family doesn't want that.

You are special even if you don't feel it.

You are loved even if you don't think it.

And

You have a purpose for living even if you haven't found it yet.

Massive blessings on you this day.

I leave this chapter with a blog post I wrote a while back.

Hope it helps

Here goes.

The pain of feeling the lowest I have ever felt in my life was sharp and heavy. My heart was in pain; my mind was in pain even my body was in pain. The heaviness was oppressive and depressive all at the same time. My world seemed like a prison. A prison with walls that slowly but relentlessly close in. I couldn't for the life of me see the good in much. I felt at times like I wasn't sure I could take much more.

I wasn't enjoying my ministry.

I wasn't enjoying life.

I spent most of my time wishing I could just walk away from everything.

Every insignificant thing seemed massive.

Every negative comment sent me to a dark, lonely place, a place where I hate to go.

I now know where this started and set in.

Without going into details that would probably make you feel sick, the control and pure stupidness of different people, people who really should have known better, yet people who let power go to their heads, had inflicted severe damage to my spirit and my soul, which in turn took its toll on my body. I had almost allowed them to do it by giving them too much power by going down the submissive route which is a dangerous thing to do if you are in the presence of people who do not understand the spiritual concept of submission. Spiritual submission is massively different to submission abuse.

I hit rock bottom after the last blow inflicted by sad, dangerous, misguided people.

This time the wound was deep and opened up a lot of other wounds I had collected in my Officership.

Depression saw its chance.

It crept up on me and seeped through those wounds and settled in to my life.

Before I became a Salvation Army Officer I still had a sense of fun, of life, and a sense of worth.

As great as my ministry seems to many people, I give all the glory to God because he has had to work through my massive weaknesses.

But underneath the inevitable acting and the false self-appearance that brings, I have been dying inside and I longed to be free.

Depression.

How do you get free from depression?

I'm not going to attempt to answer that right now for sure.

But.

I've learned some stuff.

It took a long time for me to admit that depression had set in. I just didn't want it. I convinced myself that it couldn't happen to me.

But one day.

One dark day.

I just walked into the Doctors and asked for help.

God was there.

Even though at times I wondered if he was even real.

He is amongst all the help and healing.

And

I am beginning to heal now.

It feels like I have been to hell, and I'm on the road back to Heaven.

A hell that was inflicted by others.

If you're still reading this, then I will tell you the reason that I write this condensed version of a big deal for me. I write it because I guess there are others who even now are reading between the lines of what I have written, and your own situations are surfacing right now.

Especially depression.

I am no expert on getting free of depression but know that I have learned a few things that help with recovery and felt for some reason I need to share them today.

1. Prayer is massively important, even when you feel you are speaking into thin air and getting

nothing back. Get into the lifestyle of doing it anyway. Trust God he will bring you through.

2. A verse of Scripture a day helps.
3. Admit you are struggling.
4. Do not battle it. Go to the GP.
5. If counselling is possible, go for it. A good counsellor can help you get stuff tucked away deep inside you brought out into the light. There will be forgiveness issues, that you could do with being sure about. Counsellors or Spiritual mentors are a great help in this.
6. If there is someone who is causing you distress, deal with it. If it is your boss don't leave it, tackle them. if you feel you can't speak to your boss, consider speaking to their boss.
7. Speak to a friend who you trust and share how you are feeling.
8. Don't be frightened to take time off sick if needed.
9. Don't be afraid to take medication if prescribed.

My biggest problem was having years of not doing anything but all the while getting worse.

Just deciding to deal with it by walking into the GPs Office gave me a reassuring lift.

Keeping my prayer life as strong as I could possibly maintain it, even when it felt dry, kept the hope of healing alive.

I have briefly shared this and it is hard to do, believe me. I am not the type of person who would like to read this blog post or share like this. I would rather keep it private. But I felt God wanted me to do this if only to help someone in deep need today.

So

My final word on this is.

Don't leave it any longer.

Seek help.

There is a road to recovery.

There is time to discover who you are once again.

There is hope.

Finally

A word from God.

Make your world bigger. The world that surrounds your problem or issue is surprisingly small, although you see it as insurmountable. *There is a river whose streams make glad the city of God, the holy place where the most-high dwells* (Psalm 46:6). Listen Sons and Daughters, I know about your past, present and future, head for the river that will lead you to the Holy City. Make your world bigger. Do not reside in the small world of your present circumstances. Seek the fresher air of my omnipotence. There is a bigger world waiting for you. widen your ground, seek new things, the discoveries are there, but you must find the river. I point the way. Look to Jesus. Sons and Daughters, I know you are tired of the small world, seek the Holy place, the City of God. Enlarge the place of your tent, stretch your curtains wide, do not hold back. Lengthen your cords, strengthen your stakes.

Blessings.

Self-Love

Loving yourself has had a bad press over the years.

Celebrity culture has seen to that.

People will often say about another in the times we live in, usually in a derogatory way, "He or she loves himself or herself, don't they?"

But.

Loving yourself is a thing that has got lost in this confused culture that we live in today.

Self-esteem is a much-needed trait.

But

It's hard to get.

I know I hated myself in my depression.

I hated the way I looked.

My head was too long! My weight was too massive. I hated myself.

I genuinely thought I was unattractive!

But

Then

The inside of me was a mess too.

So

All in all,

My self-esteem was off the low end of the scale!

But

How do I understand that God doesn't think those things about me when I feel so rubbish about myself?

There is the question?

Loving yourself.

Believing in yourself.

Being comfortable, or even liking being in your own company.

Are things that God genuinely wants for us?

I learned this through a precious scripture.

Do not let your adorning be external-the braiding of your hair and the putting on of gold jewellery or the clothing that you wear. But let your adorning be the hidden person of the heart with the imperishable beauty of a gentle and a quiet spirit, which in God's sight is very precious.

(1 Peter 3: 3-4)

It seems to me that God is not concerned with outward appearances.

It is an inside job he is concerned about.

This scripture suggests that beauty comes from within.

God intimates that a quiet spirit is imperishable and very precious thing to him.

So, in my recovery period from depression, I began to pray about, and work on my inner being.

I so longed for a quiet Spirit.

I so wanted to dispense with the junk of a chaotic and unsettled spirit.

I prayed every day, "Lord give me an imperishable grace, a quiet Spirit and a kind heart."

I began to work on shining this inner beauty onto others.

Then

A wonderful realization dawned on me.

I was beginning to like myself.

Love myself even.

And more than that

My self-esteem started to climb upwards.

And

I even began to miraculously be comfortable with what God has blessed me with on the outside.

So, in simple terms, of course we like to feel comfortable with our outer appearance, but that's no comfort if the inner you is a complete mess.

Not loving yourself is junk.

Scripture proves that God loves us as we are.

So

We don't have to prove ourselves to anyone.

We have no need of impressing anyone either.

It is wise to work on our inner person. The "hidden person of the heart," as this scripture puts it, in other words the beautiful inner person that God has made, often hidden within your heart, waiting to be discovered and brought out into the open.

Wow

Imagine that.

Loving ourselves?

In a quiet way!

Imagine what that would be like.

This could lead to a new and confident you.

And confidence is a gift that is waiting for you, a gift direct from God.

All of this comes from working on the inner you.

So

How about it guys.

Start working on your inner beauty.

How you speak, how you think, how you act.

Let God envelope you, let him touch your inner being with his unconditional love.

Let your spirit become quiet instead of chaotic.

A chaotic spirit is one that sees the bad in people, that wants revenge, that is jealous, that is fearful. A chaotic spirit lacks purpose and direction. A chaotic spirit is hurtful towards others, even those we love the most.

A quiet spirit allows contentment and peace to flow right through you. A quiet spirit loves, and gives, and doesn't judge.

Hey

Love yourself as God loves you.

You are incredible.

You are unique.

You are invaluable to God and to the world.

Junk

In 2013 Dawn and I were invited to speak at a prayer conference in Riga, Latvia.

We were picked up from the airport by one of the senior leaders of the Salvation Army in Latvia.

As we drove through the beautiful City of Riga, our host shared some things about the Fight that the Salvation Army had just to be active today in Latvia. She shared that the Salvation Army had been planted into the country in 1923 and had flourished as God took a hold of it. Then World War two commenced and the Soviet occupation of Latvia meant that the Salvation Army had to shut down in 1939. For fifty-one years, it lay fallow. Then, in 1990 it was re-established in the country. Today it is flourishing once again.

I was both mesmerised and completely humbled by some of the stories of the struggle these Salvationists had back then, and to some extent still have today.

As we drove down the street that the Salvation Army Corps building was located, a building that housed both the headquarters and the Riga 1 Corps, our host pointed out a massive dark bricked imposing building opposite the hall where the conference would take place. It was a foreboding place, it seemed to speak out at you, speak out control and terror. It was a former KGB headquarters, there was even a plaque in memory of the many people who entered that building and never came out again.

It kind of reached into me and I tried to imagine some of the activities that would have gone on in this building.

But

I couldn't

I couldn't even begin to imagine.

We pulled up outside Riga 1 Salvation Army Hall.

A truly magnificent Regal building.

The first thing I noticed was a huge Salvation Army flag flying furiously in the bitterly cold eastern breeze.

It hung from a flag pole fixed to the building about half way up its frontal facade.

This meant that the actual flag flew right across this street.

Now

I'm not normally a flag kind of guy.

But

The sight of this one?

With the words “Latvia for Christ,” written boldly in yellow lettering across the backdrop of a Red, Yellow and Blue Salvation Army flag touched me deeply.

This wasn’t a flag marking the site of the Salvation Army building

This was a defiant statement

A prophetic statement

That

God always wins!

What these guys had been through, is beyond comprehension, and to see something of God that could easily have been lost forever, rise again from the ashes of the Russian occupation was truly inspiring.

I was suddenly looking forward to speaking to these very special people.

I took to the platform on the Saturday evening in the first main session of the conference, and with the aid of an interpreter, began to speak.

Only

What I had prepared somehow went out of the window.

The Spirit took over.

And before I knew it I had finished my talk.

As I looked out over the hundreds of faces in front of me, people who had come from all corners of Latvia to the conference, I was suddenly so touched I was almost immobilised.

After seeing that flag flying defiantly over the City, and having heard how most of these people had absolutely nothing, yet seeing the fervent passion for Jesus written all over their faces, I had a sudden Spirit shower.

A realisation

An epic moment in my life.

I suddenly saw a lot of my junk.

For the first time, really.

Junk.

I saw the fear, the over-work, the desire to please people, the fact I couldn't say no, the stupidity of adhering to hierarchical directives, the time wasting, the hours I spent worrying over things I couldn't control, the relentless pursuit of more of me.

And

In that moment, I would say that was the first time I really knew I had to simplify my life.

Somehow.

I began to think about the defiant message of that flag, Latvia for Christ, a message that God always wins, no matter what is thrown at him, God always is victorious.

So

I began to see in my mind's eye a flag flying over my own life.

And

I knew that I had to make way more room for God in my life.

These people had been to hell and back with the Russian Army coming in and taking over. That is constantly fresh in their minds.

Yet they stand for Christ regardless.

They have a simple faith. There is nothing complicated about it.

And suddenly on stage in Riga, I craved simplicity.

My life had become too complicated.

A complex mix of battles, striving, and other junk.

I so wanted a much simpler life there and then.

My family came to mind.

I suddenly wanted to spend more time with them.

I wanted out of the Spiritual rat race.

I craved a simplicity that came down to, I love Jesus and He loves me.

And

I suspect that this is what God really craves too.

I think that is one of the most releasing thoughts in the history of time.

That Jesus loves us.

Sometimes, and I hold my hands up here too, we over-complicate things.

We do.

Theology, doctrine, differences of opinion on both of those things, as well as being edifying for some, can also make a right mess of a person.

So much so

That

The fact that Jesus loves us and desperately wants a living, breathing relationship with us, gets horribly lost in a theological quagmire.

It is just junk.

And

The reason I have written this?

Just

Know

Know that Jesus loves you.

Relentlessly

Unswervingly

He loves you.

No matter what we think of ourselves

No matter what we have done

No matter what we have hidden inside the depths of our being

Jesus loves you

That will never change

Ever

Trust

Trust brings hope.

That is a fact.

A pure, beautiful fact.

Trusting God is a skill and a belief pattern that is essential to dejunking your life.

Trusting God means that even when things do not seem possible, or, even if you can't for the life of you understand why you should do something that seems impossible or outright crazy, or, indeed if you feel you may never see the results of something you have done?

If God has spoken it?

Then you must follow your heart.

In May 1985, I was sitting in the stands at the Heysel Stadium in Brussels waiting for the European Cup Final between my team, Liverpool FC, and Juventus FC, to kick off.

All hell broke loose.

Fans clashed before the game, causing many to be injured and 39 people to lose their lives as a wall collapsed during the mayhem.

It had a massive effect on me.

And

I was ashamed of some the actions I witnessed of people from my own City, and from the City of Turin on that terrible day.

Little did I know that 20 years later in May 2005, I would be back at the Heysel Stadium as part of a delegation of Christians from Liverpool who had decided to go to the Stadium to say sorry to God on behalf of our City, and to pray for our city, and for the families of those who lost their lives in the place where these horrific events had taken place.

About Twenty of us set off for Brussels.

Dawn and I travelled to Brussels on the Eurostar. The rest of the people flew from Liverpool to Brussels, and we had arranged to meet them near the stadium.

The trouble was, no arrangements, other than where we were to meet, had been made!

We had no idea if we could get near the stadium or not. This problem was compounded as we realised an International Football Match was taking place in the stadium that very evening.

We were excited to meet up at the designated point, a restaurant near the Stadium in Brussels, but, that excitement turned into concern as we saw the people starting to gather for the match. Fans, Police, stewards, TV crews, reporters, the full caboodle, these guys were milling around the perimeter of the Stadium as the game approached.

So, we just gathered in a street and started to pray.

We prayed fervently, asking God if there was any way to get us really close to the Stadium so we could pray there, then could he do it!

As we were praying.

A very special lady, called Sue Sinclair, who was leading the group, broke away, as she had been approached by a guy in a grey suit, white crisp shirt, and an official looking tie.

She came back to us with sheer excitement on her face.

The guy had asked what we were doing?

Sue had given him the full story that we were from Liverpool, and wanted to pray for forgiveness on behalf of our City for our part in this horrible disaster 20 years earlier.

It turned out that this guy happened to be the Stadium Manager!

This guy had just been walking down this street towards the stadium.

He asked us to all follow him.

He led us to a gate right outside the stadium and asked us to wait a few minutes.

Next, a steward bedecked in his Hi-Vis yellow bib, came to the gate and asked us to follow him.

He led us through a Car parking area to a door in the stadium marked, “Entrée des joueurs,” which translated means Player’s entrance!

I couldn’t believe it!

He took us through the door of the player’s entrance, past the dressing rooms, past the treatment areas, down the tunnel that led to the pitch, and before we knew it, we out on the track surrounding the pitch in the Heysel Stadium.

The steward led us to the exact spot where the wall had collapsed killing so many innocent people all those years ago!

We started to pray, then one lady started up a song and we all started to sing a worship song to God.

As we sang.

An amazing hush came over the stadium.

A group of about a thousand stewards were seated in the stand behind us getting their instructions for the night via a guy with a loudspeaker. The guy with the loudspeaker looked around and stopped. Then stewards started taking their hats off and bowing their heads.

It was truly amazing.

Yeah.

And.

The reason I tell you this story is this.

What seemed like an impossible task, to get near the stadium that night let alone inside it?

God

Incredibly

Made

Happen!

Not only did he get us near to the stadium, he got us in, right to the spot where we needed to be.

It is amazing what trusting in God brings.

It brings hope.

Full stop.

So

Why do we so often waste space and time debating, either in our heads, or with each other, whether God can do this or do that, and then invariably think, nah, that's impossible?

Listen?

That is just junk!

Junk

Junk

Junk

Junk

Junk!!

Now to Him who is able to do immeasurably more than we dare ask or imagine, according to his power that is at work in us. (Ephesians 3:20)

These words are straight from the pages of scripture. Do we really believe this?

Do we really trust God?

Do we really trust him to do immeasurably more than we ask or imagine?

Imagine right now the scenario that you can't stop thinking about.

Imagine that Son or Daughter who you think will never know Christ?

Imagine that situation at work that is doing your head in, and you have spoken words over it like, "That will never change?"

And so on and so on!

Imagine!

Hey!

That unbelief that we harbour?

It is junk.

And

It needs dejunking.

Our unbelief.

Our mistrust.

Trust God.

Claim those words that he can do immeasurably more than we dare ask or imagine.

And

That brings?

Hope!

The hope of a saviour who is capable of the impossible.

Oh yeah

Listen

THE IMPOSSIBLE!

Don't live with the heavy junk of no hope any longer.

Allow God to shower you with hope.

It will make such a difference and will help us to shift from less of us to more of Him.

The big picture

A few years back, my Daughter Bailey was saving up money to do a gap year. Me, being daft about my daughter, felt like I wanted to do something for her.

So

I came up with this crazy plan of doing a sponsored climb.

I decided to climb up Snowdon, a 1085-meter mountain in North Wales, three times in three days!

I really had no idea what that would do to me physically, but it sounded like a clever idea.

On the first day, I got clobbered up in my walking boots and waterproof stuff as the rain was sheeting down torrentially!

I headed up the mountain with Andy, the Worship Leader, from one of our Churches in Liverpool.

One of the things I was looking forward to if we made it to the top, was the view.

I had been up Snowdon a good few times before this, but I had never ever walked up! I had always caught the train.

And

I had seen before the spectacular views that stretched for miles around, giving you a panoramic view of the world in front of you.

I was really looking forward to that.

But

Oh my!

It was not easy!

The walk I mean!

But we managed to get to the top on that first day unscathed, and although it was tough going, we felt in decent shape.

But

When we hit the summit of Snowdon on that day?

There was no view!

You could not see a thing.

All you could see was Fog.

Thick, heavy, swirling Fog.

We headed for the Café that is strategically positioned a few feet below the actual summit, and got ourselves some hot tea and a pasty each.

We sat down and spent about an hour just staring at the Fog!

Yet

As I sat and reflected, the Lord really spoke to me.

He reminded me that behind the fog there was a view.

Even though I couldn't see the view from where I was sitting, it was there.

There was a big picture even though I couldn't see it.

Psalm 53:2 says, *God looks down from Heaven on all mankind to see if there are any who understand, any who seek God.*

Looking at this gem of a verse, I realised something.

God sees the big picture.

When my spiritual life was full of Junk. This was something I just could not relate to at all. I could not see the big picture. The view of my future life was obscured by thick swirling fog that blocked out the big picture totally.

Isn't it amazing how we always want to see the big picture?

We want to have life all boxed up in a nice package.

We want to know what's around the corner, we get desperate to see what will happen next.

This kind of thinking so often causes us to constantly fail to live in the now.

It causes us to miss out on enjoying what we have now.

It robs us of the need to take care of the things we have now.

We get fretful because we don't settle for living in the now, and always crave something better that may be around the corner.

But

We can't see through the fog.

So, it drives us mad.

We know there is a bigger picture but the view is obscured.

Obscured by fog.

Spiritual fog.

God spoke to me in that mountain Café that day.

He said

"Enjoy your tea and your pasty."

"Don't worry, the big picture will always be there."

"Let me take care of that, you get that cuppa down you."

And

As I have been attempting to dejunk my spiritual life, I have found this to be an invaluable lesson.

I have started to learn to live in the now.

Probably for the first time in my entire life.

I realised what I have around me, a beautiful family, a ministry, friends, a roof over my head, food on the table you get the picture?

And

I put the bigger picture into God's hands, trusting that there was a big picture the other side of the fog.

This helped me to start enjoying life more.

Enjoying every day, enjoying the now.

When I look back on the three Churches that Dawn and I planted from scratch, I remember a time when I was particularly worried about following the vision God had given us to carry. The vision was, and still is to this day, to some extent, to initiate praying communities in the UK and beyond.

But

I was at that time, desperate to see more of the bigger picture, but the view was obscured. I could see what God wanted us to do right then, but was hungry to see more than that.

I wanted to see the future.

A very prophetic lady pulled me aside at an event I was speaking at, and for no apparent reason, because she had no idea how I was feeling, said this.

"The Spirit of God says that you are being given a whole big delicious pie, but he is only going to give you one slice at a time. Enjoy each slice as it comes."

I thought at the time she was a bit of a whacko, as I receive a massive amount of Prophetic words as I travel around, and some of them are so outrageously mad that you would laugh your head off!

But

In that moment, on the mountain, I recalled this word and I suddenly understood.

God sees the bigger picture but we won't always see it.

Corroborated greatly by 1 Corinthians 13:9 *For we know in part and we prophesy in part.*

So here is the thing

Enjoy the now.

Deal with what you have to now.

Dejunk what you need to now.

Enjoy the slice of God's pie you have been given now.

There will be more to come.

Life

Life is too short.

Linda, a beautiful lady, the amazing cook from our Prayer Centre in London, says this all the time.

If there is a disagreement in the centre, and people start to get wrapped up in it, Linda will say hey "Life is too short to worry about this."

And it's true

Very true.

Life is too short to carry junk that we don't need on our journey through life.

In the early part of this millennium, Dawn and I had a four-day break in Krakow, Poland.

It was around Christmas time and Krakow, with its historical architecture, and its Christmas Markets were looking magical.

During that visit, we had felt in our spirit that we needed to visit the former Auschwitz Concentration Camp, and I felt that the Lord had something to say to us there.

I had no idea what, but I had felt inexplicably drawn to that place.

We didn't take one of the organised tours that you can hire in the City of Krakow.

We decided to catch the train from Krakow to Oswiecim, the Polish town where the former Concentration Camp is situated.

We got off the train at Oswiecim, and it was a strange feeling, as the train station isn't really a station, it's just that the train stops on the track, and you have to jump down onto the track, and then walk across to the town.

We walked a couple of miles or so up to the entrance of Auschwitz.

As I approached the camp, I was struck by the ominous look and feel of the place. We walked along the old Judenramp, the spot where millions of Jews jumped down off the trains that were carrying them to the camp, I tried to think about how they must have felt, and for a second I felt a dread like I've never felt. I think God was allowing me a little taste of the despair that they felt so I could get a grasp of the horror I was about to learn more about inside the Camp itself. The Judenramp, now overgrown and lying silent, gave me the first taste of what God wanted to show me.

Then

We went through the famous iron entrance marked, "Albeit Macht Frei," which translated into English means,

"Work makes you free," that sick slogan that is a wrought- iron deception. My goodness, my Spirit was sad.

People must have read that and thought there may be some hope for them.

As we went to various parts of the camp, the silence and the deadness was palpable. This after all, had been a major killing ground, a territory of grave injustice, a place of unspeakable evil.

And

Those of you have been to this place?

Will know that deathly feeling you experience when you stand within its walls.

I came to a part of the camp that felt particularly dark.

It was the infamous Block Ten, where German Doctors perfomed experiments of heinous proportions on Jewish prisoners.

Very close to this foreboding red brick building was a wall that formed a kind of courtyard between the buildings situated there.

This well-built red brick wall, around fifteen-foot-high, was a place where discarded experimental prisoners were just shot and killed once they had served their purpose.

I stood against it.

I looked at the final view of the world that thousands of people would have had.

I felt pain and sorrow.

I felt fear and despair.

I also heard God speak.

This is the sentence he spoke to me.

"Life is too short."

"Life is too short to be luke-warm, life is too short to waste your time on things that really don't matter. Life is too short to harbour wounds that fester. Life is too short for misery. I came to give you life, life in all its fullness."

"Take this opportunity that I give you to love life Gary."

The tears came as some more wholeness was infused into me by the Holy Spirit.

I understood in no uncertain terms, standing in that horrendous place that Life was for living.

I was in the middle of my Officership with the Salvation Army, and my life had become laden with the heaviness of religion.

And

Here was God telling me that life is too short for that.

And

His words to me were driven home by the surroundings I was standing in.

We returned to our Hotel in Krakow, quiet, touched and determined.

Determined to change.

I had an early opportunity to think about my life further as when we flew home it turned out to be the most horrendous flight ever.

I'm not a great flyer to begin with.

I do it all the time because I have to get to places with work and holidays, but I can't say I ever enjoy it.

Usually, I am a pain on a plane, annoying Dawn Everytime a sound happens, such as a ding alerting the attendants to come, I squeeze Dawns hand and say something like, "What's that noise!" I can drive her insane on a plane, believe me!

When we reached the airport a few miles outside of Krakow, we could tell that the weather wasn't great. Then we heard that right across Europe the winds were unusually high, and they were so high in the UK that some airports were closed.

Liverpool airport wasn't closed!

Which meant that our flight was going ahead!

We boarded the plane.

It taxied out to the runway.

As the plane proceeded down the runway for take-off, you could feel the winds making the plane sway from side to side.

People were screaming.

And

That continued as we ascended into the night sky.

The whole journey, which should have taken about two and a half hours, but took four and a half hours, because the head winds were so strong, was by far and away the worst flight I have ever been on. The turbulence was violent and was battering the plane from all sides. It kept dropping leaving your stomach I the air, it was truly horrendous.

Yet.

I was calm!

It was unbelievable.

Normally I would have been beside myself with panic.

But

This time?

I was really cool about it.

We eventually landed in Liverpool safely.

As we touched down on the runway at John Lennon airport, I remember thinking how lucky I was to be alive.

Mind you so were the other two hundred passengers who were clapping their hands with relief.

I don't mean lucky to be alive because of the flight though.

I mean just blessed to be alive.

But

The word the Lord had spoken me when standing against that wall of death in Auschwitz, that life is too short, was vividly emphasised that night on that scary flight.

Life is too short.

A life full of junk, especially a spiritual life full of junk, is the great time waster.

In James 4:14 it says, *"Yet you do not know what your life will be like tomorrow. You are just vapour that appears for a little while and then vanishes away."*

So

Live in the now.

Live the present the best you can live it.

Fill the time we have been allotted with love and concern for others and with love for yourself. Fill with vision and an expanded view of life, trusting God that there is so much more than you can see.

Now is the time to offload your junk.

Now is the time to turn a corner, to take a new road, to experience life in a very unique way.

Here is a word for you.

The Spirit of God says, "Lay down your battles, your striving, your anxieties. Give them all to me. I will fight for you. You need a rest. You need time to recover your life. Loved one, I love you with a love you may never understand while you are on earth, but my heart aches for you. I want to cleanse you from all that clutters. I want to replace the junk with life abundant, replace the toxic blood with life blood everlasting. My beautiful child I know how tired you are, I know you are spent. Do not go on doing what you are doing, as it is doing you harm. Take time to rest with me, to replenish your energy, physically, mentally and spiritually. Decide, do not delay. I love you my child. I need you.

Life is too short for junk."

Postscript

So

Hey

What's your story?

How much junk are you carrying around with you?

I have shared with you some of the junk that I have carried, junk that was hindering my spiritual life.

I recognise there are so many types of junk that affect us in diverse ways individually.

This book is intended to get people to think about the junk that is affecting their spiritual lives, and then to encourage them start to dejunk.

My prayer is that you will find a way to dejunk.

I pray you will become free and light, and progress to a better quality of spiritual life, and life in general.

I am writing this part of the book on a Sunday morning in Chiswick, London, in a café overlooking Turnham Green Church.

It's 10am.

People are filing into Church ready for the 10.30am service.

And

I wonder

How much junk is being carried into Church today?

Then

I see a girl I know.

A girl Dawn and I had ministered to in when she was a Student in Durham University a few years back.

She is heading into church.

In Durham, she had been laden with guilt and shame, low self-esteem and insecurity.

Pure junk.

And

Back then she couldn't see a way out.

But today?

She is free and enjoying a better quality of life.

How?

Because she admitted to herself that she had a head full of junk.

From the minute she was truthful with herself, she was able to get rid of the various kinds of junk that stifled her relationship with Jesus.

She simplified her spiritual life

It's fitting, as I am writing the Postscript to this book, that I have seen her this morning, because she is living proof that more of God and less of us is vital to a healthy spiritual life.

She symbolises hope this day.

Yeah

Hope.

That whatever your circumstances, whatever your state of health, or state of mind, however tough your spiritual life has become, it is possible to change that.

Life is too short not to!

So

I want to finish this work with a prayer

A prayer for you.

Lord

I pray that you will touch the life of the person reading this book.

Will you breathe strength into them so that they will be able to offload the junk that holds them back from living a full life in you.

Father protect and keep them.

Shed your light onto those areas within our lives that need to be disposed of and dealt with. Make these things abundantly clear through your Spirit. Fill those spaces with your love and your power. Help us to grasp the hope that you bring, and help us to find the way forward that you have for us.

Lord I pray this book will touch the lives of many, and deposit a blessing into the whosoever.

In the name of the Father, the Son and the Holy Spirit.

Amen